Collins

English for Business

SPEAKING

James Schofield
& Anna Osborn

Collins

HarperCollins Publishers
The News Building
1 London Bridge Street
London SE1 9GF

First edition 2011
Latest Reprinted Indian edition 2016

Reprint 10 9 8 7 6 5 4 3 2

ISBN 978–93–5177–302–3

www.collinselt.com
www.collins.in

A catalogue record for this book is available
from the British Library

Typeset by Davidson Publishing Solutions, Glasgow

Printed in India by Replika Press Pvt. Ltd.

About the authors

James Schofield has worked in Asia and Europe as a Business English trainer and materials developer for over 20 years. As well as developing in-company training courses, he has written a large variety of teaching materials and regularly contributes to industry publications.

Anna Osborn has worked as a teacher and editor across Europe for more than 15 years. She has written numerous English language learning materials including business and general study books, online self-study courses and classroom workshops.

Contents

Introduction

Collins English for Business: Speaking will help you make yourself understood in business.

You can use *Speaking*:

- as a self-study course
- as a supplementary material on a business communication or business English course.

Speaking will help you develop your speaking skills in five main areas:

- Face-to-face meetings
- Telephoning
- Formal meetings and negotiations
- Presenting
- Interviews

Speaking comprises a **book** and **CD**. The **book** has 20 units.
At the back of the book there is:

- useful extra information from the Collins COBUILD Corpus about the vocabulary in the units
- the answer key
- the script for the audio recordings.

The **CD** contains over 100 tracks of audio including conversations, and listening and speaking practise activities.

Unit structure

Each of the 20 units of *Speaking* follows the same format:

Useful tips – gives you helpful advice about the communication focus of the unit

Conversation – you listen to and read a conversation or conversations. Key words and phrases are presented in bold.

Understanding – you check your understanding of the conversation.

Say it accurately – you focus on using the right words and phrases.

Say it clearly – here the focus is on pronouncing the words, phrases and sentences well.

Say it appropriately – here the focus is on tone, for example making sure you sound polite or interested.

Get speaking – these exercises give you the opportunity to practise your speaking. Often this involves interacting with a speaker on the CD in a role-play.

There are also **Grammar notes** and **Cultural notes** in the units.

Powered by COBUILD

In order to help you extend your vocabulary as you work through the material, further uses of key language are explored through references to examples taken from the Collins COBUILD Corpus. If you see this icon ⋲ next to a word in the unit, turn to the Appendix on page 84 to find more information on meaning, usage and collocations related to this word.

Using *Speaking*

You can either work through the units from Unit 1 to Unit 20, or you can pick and choose the units that are most useful to you. For example, you might want to concentrate on *Telephoning* but not spend much time on *Interviews*. The Contents pages will help you in your selection of units and your own plan for learning.

Study tips

- Each unit should take about sixty minutes to work through. Take regular breaks and do not try to study for too long. Thirty minutes is a good length for one learning session.
- Revise and go over what you have learnt regularly.
- Put the audio tracks on your mobile phone or MP3 player so you can listen to the conversations and practise activities on your way to work or when you are out jogging or walking.
- Try to find someone with whom you can practise your English, either face-to-face, over the phone or online using a webcam.
- Note down the language you find most useful.

Language level

Speaking has been written to help business learners at B1 level and above (Intermediate to Advanced).

Other titles

Also available in the *Collins English for Business* series: *Listening* and *Writing*.

Using the CD

01

This icon indicates that there is an audio track that you should listen to. Please note that the *Speaking* CD is designed for use with a computer. If you want to play the audio on a CD player, you should download the tracks to your computer and then burn all of the tracks onto an audio CD.

1 Starting a conversation

Where do you come from then?

USEFUL TIPS

- Successful small talk is not about saying brilliant things. It's about commenting on and asking about ordinary things with conviction, interest, and enthusiasm.
- Match the mood of your conversation partner. If they are smiling and cheerful, be ready to laugh. If they seem serious, be serious too.
- Ask where your partner comes from and, when somebody asks you the same thing, be ready to add something interesting about the place.
- Ask what your partner does and, when you're asked the same question, don't only give a title. Add a small piece of interesting or amusing information about the job or responsibility.

Conversations

01

Listen to extracts from four conversations heard at a conference in Marseilles.

1

A: That was really interesting what the last speaker said about opening bank accounts in the Cayman Islands.

B: Yes, it was. **So, what do you do exactly?**

A: **I'm an auditor, a forensic auditor.**

B: Ah, um, you're a forensic, um, auditor?

A: Yes, that's right.

B: Right, oh. I see. Look at the time! I must get to the next presentation...

2

C: Mmm, lovely coffee! I needed that. I just flew in from London very early this morning. **How did you get here?**

D: I came on the TGV train from Paris.

C: Really? I've never been on the TGV. **How long did that take?**

D: Oh, about four hours. But I was able to have breakfast and do some reading.

C: That sounds nice. I must try it sometime. **Marseilles's really *beautiful*, isn't it?**

D: Yes, it is. **Have you been here before?** If you haven't, you must...

3

E: ...I'm certainly looking forward to the dinner this evening.

F: I am too. Especially the fish. We don't have much fish where I live.

E: Really? **Where do you come from then?**

F: Garmisch-Partenkirchen. It's in the mountains just near Munich. What about you?

E: I'm from Cork in Ireland. The high street is supposed to have more pubs than any other town in Ireland.

F: Really? I'm going there on a business trip soon to visit the Apple factory. I must see if I can find time to visit some…

4

G: …and then I went jogging early this morning along by the sea. Fantastic sunrise coming up over the sea.

H: Really? Sunrise, you say?

G: Yes, amazing! Do you like jogging? You should try it, you know. It makes you feel really great all day long. Just set the alarm for 5.30, jump out of bed and after you've been running for about an hour or so, go back, have a shower and —

H: **Sorry, but do you know where I can smoke?** I think I want a cigarette before the next presentation. Ah, that way? Thanks.

Understanding

Look again at the conversation strategies outlined in *Useful tips*. Match the conversations to the strategies they illustrate successfully or unsuccessfully.

Conversation 1: …………………	**A** Talk about ordinary things with conviction and enthusiasm.
Conversation 2: …………………	**B** Match your mood to that of the speaker.
Conversation 3: …………………	**C** When saying where you come from, add something interesting about the place.
Conversation 4: …………………	**D** When saying what your job is, add a small piece of information about it as well.

Saying it accurately

1 **Complete the sentences with words from the box.**

looking	from	long	been	do	means	get	lovely	come	isn't

1 Have you ………………… here before?
2 Mmm, ………………… coffee! I needed that.
3 How did you ………………… here?
4 How ………………… did that take?
5 I'm a forensic auditor, which ………………… that I help banks make sure none of their staff are doing anything illegal.
6 I'm certainly ………………… forward to dinner.
7 I'm ………… Athens. It's a great place to live.

8 Marseilles's *really* beautiful, ... it?

9 So, what do you .... exactly?

10 Where do you .... from then?

2 **Alex and Sophia are attending a presentation in New York. While waiting for the speaker, they start up a conversation. Reorder their dialogue so that it makes sense.**

[ ] Alex: No, it's my first trip.

[ ] Sophia: I'm a forensic auditor, which means that I help hedge funds and banks make sure none of their staff are doing anything illegal.

[*1*] Alex: It's a beautiful day today, isn't it?

[ ] Alex: Really? And do you often find any illegal activities?

[ ] Sophia: Absolutely, I love New York in the spring. Have you been here before?

[ ] Sophia: More than you might expect! Anyway, we'd better get back to the presentation.

[ ] Alex: I'm from Athens. It's a great place to live. What do you do?

[ ] Sophia: Oh, you must visit the Guggenheim Museum and the Empire State Building. Where do you come from?

02 **3** **Listen to the audio CD to check your answers.**

4 **Complete the conversation with an appropriate question or phrase from *Saying it accurately 1*.**

Jon: This hotel is wonderfully designed, (1)..............................?

Marco: Yes, I love modern architecture. (2)..............................?

J: I'm from Dubai, home of the world's tallest building, the Burj Khalifa. And you?

M: I live in Como on the Italian lakes.

J: I've been there on holiday. It's beautiful. (3)..........................?

M: I took the train from Milan.

J: (4)..............................?

M: About four hours. It gave me a chance to catch up on some sleep!

J: (5)..............................?

M: I run a small restaurant. You'll have to stop by if you come to Como again! What about you?

J: I'm an interior designer. I mainly design the insides of shops and hotels.

M: Well, you can definitely stop by then and give me your opinion on my restaurant!

Saying it clearly

03

1 **Listen to these two questions.**

Note how the words in **bold** are connected to create new sounds.

1 So, what ***do you*** do exactly?

2 How ***did you*** get here?

2 **Listen again to the two sentences and repeat them.**

Saying it appropriately

04

1 **When starting a conversation, it is important to sound friendly and enthusiastic. Listen to the speakers and decide whether they sound friendly or unfriendly.**

1	What do you do?	friendly	unfriendly
2	Where are you from?	friendly	unfriendly
3	How did you get here?	friendly	unfriendly
4	Have you been here before?	friendly	unfriendly
5	Paris is great, isn't it?	friendly	unfriendly

05

2 **Listen again to the sentences, now said in a friendly tone, and repeat them.**

Get speaking

06

1 **You are attending the conference in Marseilles with the speakers from the dialogues at the beginning of this unit. Play the audio CD to listen to questions that your fellow delegates ask. When you hear the beep, respond with a suitable answer. Remember to follow the strategies in *Useful tips*.**

Cue *So, what do you do exactly?*

Example *I'm a journalist. I specialize in writing stories about economics and finance.*

2 **Imagine you are attending a training course at a beautiful chateau in France and you meet another attendee over lunch. Write a dialogue similar to those in *Saying it accurately 3* and *4*, showing how you might start up a conversation. Follow the example of the first question, already done for you.**

You: *This chateau is beautiful, isn't it?*

Attendee: ....

Read the dialogue aloud. If possible, record it for review.

2 Talking about jobs

It's a very challenging profession.

USEFUL TIPS: When telling people about your job:

- Be brief and precise.
- Show how your job benefits people or organizations.
- Make sure that your description is relevant to the person you are talking to.
- Avoid technical terms or acronyms unless talking to a fellow expert.
- Accentuate the positive aspects rather than the negative.

Conversation

07

Jenny Harris works for a charity organization called Foodaid. She's attending a careers fair at a university where students can talk to representatives from lots of companies to see if they would like to join them.

Student: Excuse me, are you working on the Foodaid stand?

Jenny: Yes, can I help you?

S: Well, can you tell me what jobs at Foodaid involve?

J: There are lots of jobs at Foodaid which **involve doing** all sorts of different things. What subject do you study at university?

S: Engineering.

J: Very important for Foodaid. My colleague, Hassan Sahin, for example, is a mechanical engineer and **he is responsible for helping** farmers in countries such as Chad or Pakistan where we work as an NGO to drill water wells.

S: Er... an NGO?

J: Sorry, a Non-Governmental Organization.

S: Right, of course. And what do you do?

J: Well, actually **I'm a lawyer**. **I'm in charge of managing** the legal department and we make sure that Foodaid understands any legal issues that might crop up in the work it does.

S: I hope I don't sound rude, but you look very young to do that.

J: That's what's so good about Foodaid! You get important responsibilities very quickly. A friend of mine is working in Somalia and **she manages** a development budget of about two million dollars and **she supplies** the whole of West Africa with trucks for transporting food and equipment. **It's a very challenging job** and she's only 23!

S: I see. But, as it's a charity, do you get paid for your work?

J: Yes, of course. You'll never be rich working for Foodaid, but you get paid. Very often people like you work with us for a few years to gain experience and then they move on to other jobs. Lots of companies like the fact that you've worked for a charity.

S: Hmm. So, what makes a job with Foodaid interesting, then?

J: **It's very rewarding.** You feel you are doing something useful with your skills, not just making some company shareholders rich. And even if **the work is demanding**, it's never boring.

S: It sounds really interesting. Thanks for telling me about it.

J: That's fine. Here's some more information about what we do and my card. If you have any more questions, just give me a ring...

Understanding

Look again at the strategies outlined in *Useful tips*. Which strategies does Jenny employ successfully when talking to the student? Underline the relevant parts in the conversation and note the strategy in the margin. Does Jenny make any mistakes?

Saying it accurately

1 **Match the sentences on the left with their corresponding responsibilities on the right. Follow the example.**

1 I'm a nurse.
2 I work in marketing.
3 I'm a manager on a construction site.
4 I'm a PA.
5 I'm an IT programmer.
6 I'm a project manager.
7 I'm an architect.
8 I'm a banker.

A *I'm responsible for* making sure that our projects come in on schedule and within budget.
B *My job involves managing* my customers' money effectively and profitably.
C *My company develops* websites for clients.
D *My main responsibility is* to promote new products ahead of their launch.
E *I'm in charge of designing* new buildings for our clients.
F *I help to look after* people when they are sick.
G *My job entails organizing* my boss's affairs.
H *I oversee* a team of 250 builders and twenty administrative staff.

2 **Use phrases from *Saying it accurately 1* to describe what these people do. Accentuate the positive features of each job, following the example.**

1 I'm an estate agent. *I help people find the right house to buy.*
2 I'm a lawyer. ....
3 I'm an accountant. ....
4 I'm a pediatrician. ....
5 I'm a personnel manager. ....
6 I'm a professor. ....
7 I'm an IT support manager. ....
8 I'm an entrepreneur. ....

Practise saying the sentences aloud.

3 **Complete the sentences with the verb *work*, using the correct preposition from the box. Note that in some sentences, more than one preposition is possible.**

in	with	for	to	under	as	on	a

1 I work .... a journalist. I investigate and write articles for newspapers.
2 I work .... the media. I'm an advertising executive.
3 I work .... underprivileged children, helping them to overcome disadvantages in life.
4 I work .... a multinational pharmaceutical company.
5 I work .... Lords and Sons. I'm training to be a solicitor.
6 I work .... large building projects, which often take up to two or three years to complete.
7 I work .... tight budgets and strict schedules.
8 I work .... a very inspiring manager, who has taught me everything I know.

4 **Complete the following sentences with an appropriate adjective from the box. Note that in some sentences, more than one adjective is possible.**

challenging	monotonous	rewarding	fulfilling
interesting	stressful	absorbing	demanding

1 My job doesn't vary very much on a day-to-day basis. It's quite ....
2 It's very .... to see the children's excited faces at the end of a really good lesson.
3 I find my job quite .... when my phone won't stop ringing and everyone wants to ask me something.
4 My job as an illustrator is very .... Sometimes hours go by and I don't even notice.
5 I'm always learning new things, which makes my job very .... but also very ....

Saying it clearly

08 **1** **Listen to the adjectives from *Saying it accurately 4* and mark the stressed syllable of each word, following the example.**

1 <u>cha</u>llenging
2 monotonous
3 rewarding
4 fulfilling
5 interesting
6 stressful
7 absorbing
8 demanding

2 **Listen again to the adjectives and repeat them.**

Saying it appropriately

09

1 **Listen to the eight speakers from *Saying it accurately 1* talking about their jobs. Circle the correct words in this sentence.**

The speakers are very enthusiastic/unenthusiastic, which helps them to accentuate the positive/negative aspects of their jobs.

2 **Listen again to the sentences and repeat them.**

Get speaking

1 **Your old school or college has approached you and asked you to send them a short recording describing your job. It will be played to students who are interested in following your chosen field.**

- Briefly explain what you do, using appropriate adjectives.
- Make it relevant to the students listening.
- Accentuate the positive aspects of your profession.

Record yourself if possible. Then, review your recording and consider how you can improve. Repeat the exercise.

2 **Imagine that a work experience person is visiting your office and is asking each employee *'What do you do?'* How would you answer? Practise your answer aloud, using the correct tone. How would your colleagues describe their jobs? Imagine their answers and practise them aloud. If possible, record yourself for review.**

Grammar note

Note how we use the *-ing* form after *involve, be responsible for,* and *be in charge of.*

Examples from the text:

There are lots of jobs at Foodaid which *involve doing* all sorts of different things.

He *is responsible for helping* farmers.

I'm *in charge of managing* the legal department.

My job *involves providing* people with the computer equipment they require.

I'm responsible for overseeing the production of all our fashion lines.

He's in charge of bringing in as many advertisements as possible for our magazine.

3 Showing interest in other people

Oh, I know what you mean.

USEFUL TIPS: When you are in conversation:

- Echo the key information to encourage further explanation, for example, *I'm allergic to shellfish. To shellfish?*
- Empathize. Use phrases to show that you understand how your partner feels, for example, *That's amazing!* or *Really?*
- Paraphrase. Reformulate in your own words what has been said to show that you are listening, for example, *So what you're telling me is...*

Conversation

10 **Emily is having lunch in the company canteen with a new team member, Casper.**

Casper: It's a very different way to do business here in Singapore, compared to Germany.

Emily: **I know what you mean.** Do you find it difficult?

C: No, not at all. It's interesting.

E: Interesting?

C: Yes. For example, in Singapore you discuss prices much earlier in a negotiation than we do in Germany.

E: **Really? So, you mean that** you leave price negotiations till the end of a discussion?

C: Oh, yes. In Singapore you start talking about prices for products when in Germany we're still trying to define exactly what's wanted.

E: **How amazing!** I didn't realize. I suppose we think it's a waste of time discussing something if the price is always going to be unrealistic.

C: **I see.**

E: Whereas in Germany you feel you can't begin to think about price until you know all the details.

C: **That's right.**

E: So, do you like Singapore?

C: Oh, yes. Very much, especially the food. But I need to do some sport. I've put on two kilos already! Back in Berlin I play centre forward for the company football team.

E: **Really?**

C: Yes, um... anyway, um...

E: Do you notice any other differences between business life here and in Germany?

C: Well, another difference is the flexibility that a manager has here.

E: Flexibility?

C: Yes. In Germany it's very difficult to be a manager because every time you want to introduce a change in the organization or in communication processes, you have to ask the Workers' Council for permission. This makes innovation very slow, which isn't good for the employees at all.

E: **So, what you're saying is** that the Workers' Council in Germany makes things more difficult for employees, not easier.

C: Sometimes, yes.

E: **That's terrible!**

Saying it accurately

1 **Complete the phrases with words from the box.**

saying	that's	mean	how	really	other	know	terrible

To show empathy

1 I .... what you mean.
2 ....?
3 That's ....!
4 .... so true.
5 .... amazing!

To paraphrase

6 So in .... words...
7 So what you're .... is...
8 So you .... that...

2 **Group these expressions that show empathy under the correct heading, following the example.**

1 That's wonderful!
2 How terrible!
3 Fantastic!
4 That's unbelievable!
5 That's awful!
6 How amazing!
7 Great!
8 Oh no!
9 How incredible!
10 That's dreadful!

To show empathy about something good: *1*
To show empathy about something bad:
To show disbelief:

3 **Rachel uses all three strategies to show interest in what Tess says. Number Rachel's responses to Tess's statements. Each time, note the strategy Rachel uses.**

Tess: I feel terrible.

1 *Echoing*

Tess: I've got such a headache.

2 ....

Tess: I think it was brought on by sitting in a car for three hours.

3 ....

Tess: Yes, it took me three hours to travel ten kilometres.

4 ....

Tess: I know, but at least I'm here now. And I've got some exciting news!

5 ....

Tess: Yes, I've been promoted!

6 ....

Tess: Uh-huh, it happened while you were away.

7 ....

Tess: That's right! And it means I get a pay rise and a company car!

8 ....

[ ] Rachel: How awful!

[*1*] Rachel: Terrible?

[ ] Rachel: That's unbelievable!

[ ] Rachel: So what you're saying is I went on holiday for a week and come back to find you're a senior manager?!

[ ] Rachel: You mean that you were stuck in traffic for three hours!

[ ] Rachel: Really?

[ ] Rachel: Promoted?

[ ] Rachel: How amazing! Congratulations!

Saying it clearly

11

1 **Listen to these three extracts from the conversations.**

Note how Emily and Rachel show interest.

Casper: *No, not at all. It's interesting.*

Emily: *Interesting?*

Tess: *I feel terrible.*

Rachel: *Terrible?*

Tess: *Yes, I've been promoted!*

Rachel: *Promoted?*

2 **Listen again and repeat the echoing comments, using the same intonation.**

Saying it appropriately

12

1 **Emily's preferred topic of conversation – ways of doing business or football – is implied by her intonation. Compare the way that she says the word *really* in these two extracts. Then circle the correct words in the following sentences.**

In the first extract, Emily's tone is keen/uninterested and her intonation is rising/falling. This response encourages Casper to continue/stop talking about the topic.

In the second extract, Emily's tone is keen/uninterested and her intonation is rising/falling. This response encourages Casper to continue/stop talking about the topic.

13 **2** **Listen again. Play the audio CD to start. When you hear the beep, say *really* in a way that shows interest and enthusiasm.**

14 **3** **When you express empathy, it's important to use an enthusiastic tone of voice. Listen to the phrases from *Saying it accurately 2*. Tick those where the speaker sounds as though she means what she is saying.**

1 That's wonderful!
2 Fantastic!
3 How amazing!
4 Great!
5 How terrible!
6 That's awful!
7 Oh no!
8 That's dreadful!
9 That's unbelievable!
10 How incredible!

15 **4** **Listen again to the phrases, now all said with an appropriate tone, and repeat them.**

Get speaking

16 **1** **Your boss has asked to talk to you. Play the audio CD to start. When you hear the beep, pause and respond suitably.**

1 Empathize with your boss.
2 Echo what he says.
3 Paraphrase what he says.
4 Agree with him.

17 **2** **Play the audio CD to start. When you hear the beep, pause and respond with a suitable expression. Follow the example.**

For example, you hear: *We've decided to give you an enormous bonus this year.*

You say: *An enormous bonus?* or *That's fantastic!*

Try to use all three strategies – *echoing, empathizing* and *paraphrasing* – during the exercise.

4 Exchanging information

I heard it on the grapevine.

USEFUL TIPS: Here are three ways to get the information you want within your organization:

- First offer appropriate information yourself. If you want to find out about a particular area, offer information of your own first to show you can be trusted. Think carefully about what information is appropriate to pass on to others.
- Ask questions indirectly. If you want to ask about somebody or something, use statements with question tags rather than direct questions, for example, *You know John, don't you?* rather than *Do you know John?* A direct question may frighten someone into remaining silent but a statement that sounds more like speculation will often be confirmed or corrected by somebody with better information.
- Create intimacy. If you don't know somebody very well, but want to exchange information with that person, you can use these techniques: Drop their name into conversation more than usual and use *we*, *us* and *our* as often as possible, for example, *I think **we**'re going to see a lot of changes in **our** department soon, **Peter**.*

Conversation

18

Michael is driving with his colleague, Candy, to a meeting. They are talking about a colleague of theirs, Christine.

Candy: I really want to thank you, Michael, for taking me with you to the meeting. I just can't get used to driving on the left!

Michael: No problem.

C: You used to work for our new chief legal officer, Christine Bender, didn't you?

M: Yes, that's right. She and I started together in the legal department five years ago. Then I changed over to IT.

C: Christine is so successful. She did an amazing job for us dealing with that whole corruption scandal last year, don't you think?

M: Yes, she did. But, **between you and me,** Christine could never have managed that without her team.

C: That's so true, Michael. She always picks good people to work with her. By the way, **I heard on the grapevine** that she's going to move to our New York office next.

M: Yes, I heard that too. **I wonder how** her husband feels about it. He's a journalist, I think.

C: Well, **according to** Christine's assistant, Mrs Weber, that's not a problem. He's going to write articles about New York nightlife. Although **I can't imagine** who's going to look after the children then.

M: **Apparently**, they're going to have a nanny. **I overheard** Christine talking to the boss about it this morning. It must be very expensive, but they'll have enough money.

C: **I suppose** they might appoint somebody from Christine's team to carry on her work.

M: Ah, no! **It seems that** Christine didn't want to recommend any of them to the boss, so Gabriele from the commercial department will take over. Christine's team was really angry!

Understanding

Look again at the strategies outlined in *Useful tips*. Candy uses all three to get information from Michael. Underline the relevant parts in the conversation and note the strategy that she uses in the margin.

Saying it accurately

19

1 Imagine you work with Candy and Michael. They both have information they want to share with you. Listen to their statements and answer these questions.

1 Who sounds as though they are passing on information based on fact?

....

2 Who sounds as though they are passing on information that may be unreliable?

....

2 Tick the phrases that show that your information is based on what you've *heard on the grapevine*, rather than what you *know*. Follow the example.

According to Jane, ... ✓
I'm sure that...
I overheard Ben saying...
Apparently, ...
I'm convinced that...
I heard on the grapevine that...
It's certain that...
It seems/appears that...
By all accounts, ...
...so I'm told.
It's guaranteed that...
Did you hear that...?
I heard that...

3 Complete the following sentences with words or phrases from *Saying it accurately 2.* Make it clear that these are simply reports that you have heard on the grapevine. Try to use each phrase only once.

1 .... the section manager is going to resign tomorrow.
2 She's been for interviews at other companies, ...
3 She hasn't been happy here for a while, ...
4 ....she wants to work abroad.
5 .... she'll be gone by January.
6 .... her secretary, the board isn't going to replace her internally.
7 .... they are planning to restructure her division?
8 .... they will combine the two departments so that they can make cutbacks.

4 **Read these answers. Write statements creating a sense of intimacy with the speaker. Follow the example.**

1 Find out if Jay has spent time in the Washington office.
'You've spent time in our Washington office, haven't you, Jay?'

2 Check that Rachel approved the new brochure before it was sent to the printers.
....

3 Find out if Matt knows the new CEO.
....

4 Ask if Lianne is attending the conference this year.
....

5 Find out if Dan has seen the budget for next year.
....

Saying it clearly

20 **1** **Listen to these sentences.**

Note how the words that imply that you are passing on rumours rather than fact are stressed to reinforce this message.

Apparently, *the section manager is going to resign tomorrow.*

She's been for interviews at other companies, ***so I'm told.***

2 **Listen again to the sentences and repeat them, using the correct stress.**

Saying it appropriately

21 **1** **Listen to these questions and decide whether the speakers are being direct or intimate. Note how the speakers create a sense of intimacy by using a light, friendly tone of voice and the strategies outlined in *Useful tips.***

question 1	direct	intimate
question 2	direct	intimate
question 3	direct	intimate
question 4	direct	intimate
question 5	direct	intimate
question 6	direct	intimate

22 **2** **Listen to the questions, now all phrased to create a sense of intimacy, and repeat them.**

Get speaking

23

1 **You've heard that the company is planning to set up a sports and social committee. Start a conversation with Max, the personnel manager, to try to find out more about it. Play the audio CD and follow the cues. You start.**

1 Tell Max the rumour that you heard.
2 Ask indirectly if he knows about it.
3 Tell him that the CEO's secretary, Janice, told you that the CEO was very enthusiastic about it.
4 Ask indirectly if he knows when the meeting might happen.
5 Ask indirectly if he would want to be involved.

2 **What sort of information is passed around your workplace? Write a short conversation based on the dialogue at the beginning of this unit, being the kind of discussion that might take place in your office. Try to incorporate all the strategies from this unit. Then read it aloud, practising your pronunciation. Record it if possible, for review.**

Grammar note

Compare the two predictions for the future of Christine's role and note how the use of *I suppose they might* indicates speculation and *will* implies certainty.

Examples from the text:

I suppose they might appoint somebody from Christine's team to carry on her work.
Gabriele from the commercial department *will* take over.

I suppose we might employ some more staff.
We'll employ some more staff.

Cultural note

If you are working in international teams, you will need to find out the best way to get information from colleagues. It may be that there is not a lot of office gossip and that it is inappropriate to talk about individuals in the way the people do in the dialogues in this unit. Privacy may be an important part of the culture.

5 Cold calling

Do you have a moment to speak to me?

USEFUL TIPS: When cold calling (approaching prospective clients or customers for the first time), keep the following points in mind:

- Be clear and concise about who you are and the purpose of the call.
- Use questions to help and guide the person you are calling.
- Always use titles (such as Dr, Mr, and Ms) and never first names.
- Don't be offended by hostile behaviour. It's not personal.

Conversation

24 **Macey Chance is on the phone, trying to set up meetings to discuss her company's services.**

Macey C: This is Macey Chance from Turner & Young Consultants. Am I speaking to Mr Given?

Speaker 1: No.

Mr H: Trancross Power and Gas, project management office.

MC: Good morning. **Am I speaking to** Mr Harvey?

Mr H: Speaking.

MC: Oh hello, Mr Harvey. **This is Macey Chance from** Turner & Young Consultants.

Mr H: Oh, yes.

MC: **Do you have a moment to speak to me?**

Mr H: Um... well, yeah.

MC: Thank you. **My company specializes in** helping power industry companies manage risk, Mr Harvey. **Do you think that's something that might be of interest to you?**

Mr H: Er... well, we have risk management plans in place, you know.

MC: I'm sure! But **may I ask you a question**, Mr Harvey? Do you have plans in place for handling risks generated by climate change?

Mr H: Um, it depends on what you mean exactly. Of course, we have plans in place for damage to our power plants from bad weather.

MC: Well, managing short-term risk is very important of course. But **would you like to find out about** ways to manage risk caused by long-term adjustments to weather patterns? I'm talking about global warming and the impact that will have on energy supplies.

Mr H: Um, that's very unpredictable, isn't it?

MC: Yes, you're quite right, Mr Harvey. And very risky. That's why my company specializes in designing plans that minimize the risks for companies like yours. **Would it be possible to arrange a meeting where I could explain** our services in more detail?

Mr H: Well, it could be interesting.

MC: Fine. **When's a good time for you,** Mr Harvey?

Mr H: Er, let me just check my appointments. Um, how about Friday this week, 2 p.m.?

Understanding

Read the following stages of the dialogue and put them into the correct order.

[ ] She explains what her company specializes in and the reason for her call.

[*1*] Macey Chance checks that she is speaking to the correct person.

[ ] She sets up a meeting to discuss the matter further.

[ ] She introduces herself and says where she works.

[ ] She asks questions to gauge the person's interest.

[ ] She checks that the person she is speaking to has time to talk.

Saying it accurately

1 **Unscramble the words to form sentences to use when cold calling.**

A think / interest / you / you / something / be / that / of / Do / that's / to / might

....?

B set / Mr Lee / Could / meeting / week / we / up / a / for / next

....?

C specializes / bespoke software / My / in / company / designing

....

D Tom Sweeney / Lermans and Co / is / from / This

....

E question / May / Mr Lee / ask / you / I / a

....?

F moment / you / have / Do / a / speak / me / to / to

....?

2 **Complete the conversation with sentences from *Saying it accurately 1*. Write the correct letter in the space provided.**

Tom Sweeney: Is that Mr Lee?

Mr Lee: Speaking.

TS: (1) ....

Mr Lee: Uh-huh.

TS: (2) ....

Mr Lee: I suppose so, yes, go ahead.

TS: (3) ....

Mr Lee: I see.

TS: (4) ....

Mr Lee: Yes, it sounds interesting.

TS: (5) .... Are you currently using software that doesn't fully meet your business's needs?

Mr Lee: Well, yes we have had some issues with it this year.

TS: (6) ....

Mr Lee: Yes, I'd be interested to hear more.

3 **Match the questions from the conversation on the left to those on the right that serve the same purpose.**

1 Am I speaking to Mr Harvey?

2 Do you have a moment to speak to me?

3 Would you like to find out about ways to manage risk caused by long-term adjustments to weather patterns?

4 Would it be possible to arrange a meeting next week where I could explain our services in more detail?

5 When's a good time for you, Mr Harvey?

A When is convenient for you, Mr Harvey?

B Could we set up a meeting next week to discuss it further?

C Is that Mr Harvey?

D Is this a good time?

E Would you be keen on finding out more about ways to manage risk caused by long-term adjustments to weather patterns?

Saying it clearly

25

1 **Listen to these two questions from *Saying it accurately 1*.**

Do you have a moment to speak to me?

Note that when a word ends with a consonant and the next word begins with the same consonant, we do not repeat the sound, but pronounce them together.

*Could we set up a meeting nex(**t**) week to discuss it further?*

Note that when the sound 't' appears between two consonants, it sometimes disappears altogether. This is known as elision.

2 **Listen again to the sentences and repeat them.**

Saying it appropriately

26

1 **When approaching potential customers over the phone, it's important to use the right tone of voice. Listen to the sentences from *Saying it accurately 1* and choose the adjective describing the speaker's tone of voice.**

1 polite or pushy? (too forceful)

2 enthusiastic or bored?

3 abrupt or friendly?

4 pushy or friendly?
5 bored or polite?
6 bored or friendly?

27 **2** **Listen to the sentences again, now all said in a positive, appropriate manner, and repeat them.**

Get speaking

28 **1** **You are a salesperson at Top Tier Training and you call Frederic Gulbert, personnel manager at Rogers and Co. Your aim is to set up a meeting with him to discuss your range of services. Play the audio CD and follow the cues. You start.**

1 Check that you are speaking to Frederic Gulbert.
2 Say who you are and who you work for.
3 Check that Frederic has time to talk to you now.
4 Explain that your company specializes in providing motivational training courses for staff and gauge his interest.
5 Suggest a meeting for 10 a.m. next Tuesday.

28 **2** **Repeat the activity from *Get speaking 1*. This time, however, imagine you are calling Frederic Gulbert as a representative of your own company. Explain what your company specializes in and gauge his interest in your products or services. Play the audio CD and follow the cues. You start.**

Grammar note

Note how we use the -ing form after specialize in, focus on, and concentrate on.

Examples from the text:

My company *specializes in designing* plans…

This team *specializes in providing* the best service for customers.

My job is to *focus on cutting* costs wherever possible.

Our personnel department *concentrates on recruiting* the very best people for the company.

Cultural note

Cold calling is an accepted way of doing business in many cultures. However, in some cultures, business contacts will usually be initiated through referrals, for example *Astra Purim suggested I get in touch with you about…* . Whatever your situation, a referral will always help you make contact with people. When cold calling across cultures, make sure you find out first whether this approach is culturally appropriate.

6 Confirming or rearranging appointments

I look forward to seeing you then.

USEFUL TIPS: Once you have fixed your appointment with a business partner, telephone a couple of days beforehand to confirm the details of your meeting. Keep the following points in mind:

- Confirm the topic, date, time, and place.
- Be ready with alternative appointment times if the original time has to be changed.
- Check to see if the customer has any new requests.

Conversations

29

Robbie Taylor is confirming his appointments for next week.

1

Sabine G: Sabine Gerland.

Robbie T: Hello, Ms Gerland. This is Robbie Taylor from Queensfield Ltd. How are you?

SG: Fine, thanks. And you?

RT: Very well. **I'm just ringing to confirm our appointment for Tuesday afternoon at 3 p.m.** to discuss our project management services for the Potsdam project.

SG: Yes, that's right. I'm looking forward to it.

RT: **Can I just check the address? That's Quiddestrasse 14, isn't it?**

SG: Er, no, Quiddestrasse 40.

RT: Right, 40, OK. And **could you spell Quidde for me?**

SG: Of course. That's Q-U-I-D-D-E. If you go to our website, you'll find full directions.

RT: Right. Thanks. So, **I look forward to seeing you then.**

2

RT: Queensfield Ltd. Robbie Taylor.

Gerhard S: Oh hi, this is Gerhard Schmidt calling from Hipax in Berlin.

RT: Oh, hello Mr Schmidt. How are you?

GS: I'm fine, thank you. And you?

RT: I'm well, thanks.

GS Good. I'm afraid I have to cancel our meeting next Tuesday morning. I'm going to be away visiting one of our key customers.

RT: **No problem. Would Wednesday afternoon be more convenient?**

GS: Unfortunately not. One colleague I wanted to come to our meeting will be in Paris and I'll be in Munich.

RT: I see. Well, **would you like me to arrange a telephone conference** instead?

GS: Mmm, that's a good idea. We're both free at 2 p.m. on Wednesday. Will you email me the details?

RT: Of course. Actually, I wanted to call you anyway, Mr Schmidt. **Would you or your colleagues be interested in any of our other project management services, like logistics, for example?**

Understanding

This is how Robbie Taylor's diary looked before his two phone calls. Make any necessary changes to it.

Tuesday		**Wednesday**	
9 a.m.		9 a.m.	
10 a.m.		10 a.m.	*Gerhard Schmidt, Hipax, Berlin*
11 a.m.		11 a.m.	
12 p.m.		12 p.m.	
2 p.m.		2 p.m.	
3 p.m.	*Sabine Gerland, Quiddestrasse 14*	3 p.m.	
4 p.m.		4 p.m.	
5 p.m.		5 p.m.	

Saying it accurately

1 **Complete the sentences with words from the box.**

spell	confirm	forward	teleconference	check	better

1 I'm just ringing to .... our appointment for Friday morning at 9 a.m.
2 Can I just .... the address?
3 Could you .... that for me?
4 That's not a problem. Would Thursday afternoon be .... for you?
5 Would it help if I arranged a .... ?
6 I look .... to seeing you then.

2 **Match the sentences on the left with those on the right that have a similar purpose. Follow the example.**

1 I'm just ringing to confirm our appointment for Tuesday afternoon at 3 p.m.

2 Can I just check the address?

3 No problem. Would Tuesday afternoon be more convenient?

4 Would you like me to arrange a telephone conference?

5 Would you be interested in any of our other services?

A Could you just confirm where your offices are?

B Shall I organize a telephone conference?

C I'm just calling to check that it's still convenient for us to meet on Friday at 10 a.m.

D Can I interest you in any other services that we provide?

E That's fine. How about Friday morning instead?

Saying it clearly

30

1 **Listen to the five sentences on the right from *Saying it accurately* 2.**

I'm just calling to check that it's still convenient for us to meet on Friday at 10 a.m. ↗

Note how the speaker's voice goes up, even when it is not a question.

2 **Listen again to the sentences and repeat them.**

Saying it appropriately

31

When your business partners contact you regarding an appointment, remember to be polite, flexible and to respond to their needs. Your phone is ringing. Listen to four sentences from the same conversation. Play the audio CD to start. When you hear the beep, pause and respond, choosing a suitable answer.

1

A Fine, thanks. And you?

B I've had better days. And you?

C I woke up with terrible backache and it hasn't really lifted even though I've taken lots of painkillers. And you?

2

A That's a shame. Never mind, maybe some other time.

B No problem. Would Wednesday be more convenient?

C Oh really? It's just that I'm really busy next week and that's the only time I'm free.

3

A Well, maybe we'll leave it till she gets back.

B Does she really need to be there?

C I see. Would you like me to arrange a telephone conference?

4

A Excellent, I'll email you with the details. Would you be interested in any of our other services?

B I look forward to seeing you on Tuesday, then.

C Can I just check the spelling of that?

Get speaking

32 **1 You are the customer relations manager for Marlow Construction. Look at two of your diary entries for next week and then make the phone calls to confirm your appointments. Play the audio CD to start. When you hear the beep, pause and respond.**

Wednesday	10 a.m.	*Giovanni Fabro, 40 Findon Street – discuss Westdene Hospital building contract*
Thursday	3 p.m.	*Joy Lee, 20 South Road – update on Queen's Hotel building project*

The call to Giovanni

1 Greet him, say who you are and where you work, and ask how he is.
2 Respond to Mr Fabro's question and explain the reason for your call.
3 Check that you have the correct address.
4 Ask him to spell it for you and make notes accordingly.
5 Thank him and end the call politely.

The call to Joy

6 Greet her, say who you are and where you work, and ask how she is.
7 Respond to Ms Lee's question and explain the reason for your call.
8 Respond appropriately and suggest an alternative time to meet.
9 Respond appropriately and end the call politely.

33 **2 Think about your workplace. You have a meeting booked on Monday at 4 p.m. with Valerie Auguste. Play the audio CD to start. When you hear the beep, pause and respond. Remember to be flexible, suggesting an alternative time or a telephone conference where appropriate. You start.**

Cultural note

When making or receiving a business call, you may be expected to engage in some small talk at the beginning of the conversation. Look again at Robbie Taylor's two conversations to see how he makes his telephone partners feel at ease by using the phrase *How are you?* The answer should be brief and positive (even if this is not, in fact, the case), for example, *Very well.* or *I'm fine, thank you.* You may wish to reciprocate by asking, *And you?*

7 Making a complaint on the telephone

I'm afraid I need to make a complaint.

USEFUL TIPS: When making a complaint, keep the following points in mind:

- Make sure you are speaking to the person who is in a position to help you. Ask questions to check who exactly you are talking to and take notes.
- Stay as unemotional as possible. Blaming the person you are calling will not help. Separate the problem from the person. Be firm, but polite.
- State the problem clearly and calmly. Include as much relevant detail as possible, including names, times, places, previous contacts, and so on.
- State exactly what you want the person you are calling to do.
- Check when you can expect results/feedback from the person you are speaking to.

Conversation

34

Andrea King is phoning Alpine Executive Events to make a complaint.

Receptionist: Alpine Executive Events Ltd, London. Priti Makesch speaking. How can I help you?

Andrea K: Good morning, my name is Andrea King. I'm the HR manager for Carabella Hotels. **Could I speak to your supervisor, please?**

R: Can I ask what it's regarding?

AK: **I need to make a complaint.**

R: I'll just put you through to Mr Mendip. One moment, please.

George M: Good morning, Ms King. How can I help?

AK: Good morning. **Could you tell me your name and position, please?**

GM: Of course, my name's George Mendip and I'm responsible for customer relations.

AK: Thank you, Mr Mendip. **I'll just make a note of that.** I hope you can help me. I'm currently attending your team-building training course in Wales with a team of our managers.

GM: The 'Big T' course. Very popular.

AK: Well, **I'm afraid I'm not satisfied with** the performance of your trainer, David Llewellyn.

GM: Oh dear. What seems to be the problem?

AK: He's very unhelpful and doesn't explain himself properly.

GM: How do you mean?

AK: Well, he talks extremely fast and makes all the instructions very complicated. And if you ask him a question, he just says he's already explained it. I tried to talk to him about the problem, but he didn't take me seriously at all. The situation is entirely unsatisfactory.

GM: I see... Well, I'm sorry to hear that, but I'm not sure what I can do.

AK: **I'd like you to** telephone Mr Llewellyn immediately and explain that we want much clearer explanations and support for tomorrow's tasks.

GM: Well, OK, I could give him a ring.

AK: And **could you let me know when you have** spoken to him, please?

GM: Yes, I will.

AK: **When will you get back to me?** Do you have my number?

GM: I think so... Yes, I do. I'll get back to you by, um, the end of today.

AK: Many thanks. I really appreciate your help on this.

GM: Not at all.

Understanding

Match the following strategies to the corresponding sentences from the telephone conversation.

Confirm when your expectations will be met.

Make sure you're speaking to the person who can help you.

Set out your expectations to solve the problem.

State your complaint.

Strategy	Sentences from the telephone conversation
	• Could I speak to your supervisor, please? • Could you tell me your name and position, please? I'll just make a note of that.
	• I need to make a complaint. • I'm afraid I'm not satisfied with...
	• I'd like you to...
	• Could you let me know when you have... ? • When will you get back to me?

Saying it accurately

1 **Unscramble the words to form sentences to use when making a complaint.**

1 this product / satisfied / I'm sorry / with / not / to / I'm / that / say

....

2 appears / this product / with / problem / There / to / a / be

....

3 not / all / this service / I'm / with / at / happy

....

4 seem / concerns / to / regarding / There / be / some / this / product

....

5 replace / Please / you / could / it

.... ?

6 today / ensure / you / replacement / that / sent / the / Would / is

.... ?

7 email / me / sent / when / Would / has been / be / to / able / you / it

.... ?

8 can / you / expect / I / When / hear / to / from

.... ?

2 **Underline adjectives that might be useful for making a complaint and describing a product or service.**

damaged	poor	so-so	unsatisfactory
defective	passable	indifferent	unsuitable
delayed	high quality	unacceptable	
disappointing	inadequate	unprofessional	
tolerable	mediocre	unreasonable	

3 **Rank these adverbs according to how forceful they make a complaint.**

The situation is ***entirely*** *unsatisfactory.* (forceful)

The situation is ***somewhat*** *unsatisfactory.* (not so forceful)

absolutely	quite	somewhat	entirely
altogether	rather	totally	
considerably	slightly	utterly	
extremely	completely	very	

4 **Using the prompts, make complaints and set out your expectations as to how each problem can be resolved. Follow the example.**

conference venue (forceful complaint)

I'm not at all happy with *the conference venue because it's* ***entirely inadequate*** *for our needs.* ***Please could you*** *find an alternative venue right away?*

1 latest sales figures (not so forceful)
2 latest delivery (forceful)
3 budget for the new project (forceful)
4 accounts system (not so forceful)
5 new catering company (forceful)

Saying it clearly

35

1 **Listen to these forceful complaints, noting the syllable stress.**

1 *It's absolutely unacceptable.*
2 *It's altogether unreasonable.*
3 *It's completely unprofessional.*
4 *It's entirely unsuitable.*
5 *It's utterly inadequate.*
6 *It's totally unsatisfactory.*

2 Listen again to the sentences and repeat them.

Saying it appropriately

36 **1** It's very important that you remain calm when making a complaint. Do not blame the person you are speaking to. Listen to the following speakers and decide whether their complaints are phrased appropriately or inappropriately.

speaker 1	appropriately	inappropriately
speaker 2	appropriately	inappropriately
speaker 3	appropriately	inappropriately
speaker 4	appropriately	inappropriately
speaker 5	appropriately	inappropriately

37 **2** Listen to the complaints, now phrased appropriately, and repeat them.

Get speaking

38 **You are the CEO of a small firm, Rickmans and Co., and you have been badly let down by your IT support company, Lettermans International, so you telephone to complain. First, read about the problem and your proposed solution. Then play the audio CD to start. When you hear the beep, pause and respond.**

The problem

Lettermans have recently installed new IT systems, which your employees are finding very difficult to master because they received insufficient training. Also, Lettermans agreed to provide a 24-hour support line and this has proved unreliable.

Your proposed solution

You would like Lettermans to provide additional training for employees and ensure that their support line is staffed 24 hours a day, as agreed.

1 Explain who you are, where you work, and whom you would like to speak to.
2 Explain the reason for your call.
3 Ask for the speaker's name and position.
4 Make a point of writing down her name and say that you hope that she can help.
5 Explain the exact nature of your complaint, using an introductory phrase and a suitable adjective and adverb.
6 Explain how she can improve the situation.
7 Ask her to let you know when the problem has been addressed.
8 Check when this will be.
9 Thank her for her help.

8 Dealing with a complaint on the telephone

Oh dear, I'm sorry to hear that.

USEFUL TIPS: When dealing with a complaint, keep the following points in mind:

- Let the caller express their complaint. Don't interrupt, but try to get all the details. Take notes.
- Once they have finished complaining, summarize the complaint, clarify any unclear details and show empathy.
- Apologize. Do not try to make excuses but provide an explanation if the customer requests one.
- State what you are going to do to resolve the situation.
- Tell the customer when they can expect results/feedback.
- Stay calm with the customer at all times. Separate the problem from the person.

Conversation

39

Tony Hopps is phoning Kelly Masterman at Argonaut Mediterranean Cruises to make a complaint.

Kelly M: Argonaut Mediterranean Cruises Ltd.

Tony H: Ah, this is Tony Hopps here. Is that Kelly Masterman, the general manager?

KM: Speaking.

TH: Ah, right. Well, you listen here, Ms Masterman. I've just arrived home from one of your eastern Mediterranean cruise ships – Queen of the Waves – and I'm not at all happy. I've got a whole list of complaints.

KM: **Oh dear, I'm sorry to hear that.** Let me just get a pen and I'll note them down. Right, **can you give me the details?**

TH: Well, first of all, we booked an expensive cabin on the outside of the ship. But there was a problem with that cabin and there were no others available on the outside. So we had to have one in the middle of the ship and my wife spent three days feeling really seasick. Then, for the buffet lunch, it was supposed to be an all-you-can-eat buffet, but when we got there at 2 p.m. we found that there were only a few bits of cheese and salad left for us. And then, in the programme for Saturday evening, it said there was a fancy-dress party. So we dressed up, but we found that everybody else was just in jeans and T-shirts. It was so embarrassing!

KM: Oh, **you must have felt terrible!**

TH: Yes, we did. And finally, I sent my costume to the ship's laundry to be cleaned and it got lost. That really was the last straw!

KM: **So, let me just recap.** In a nutshell, you didn't get the cabin you ordered, the buffet lunch was finished by the time you got there, the fancy-dress party listed in the programme didn't take place, and your costume was lost.

TH: That's right.

KM: Well, first of all, we're not going to try to pass the buck here, so **we would like to apologize to you for** these problems. This is what I propose: I'm going to call the ship and see if I can find out what was going on. Can I call you back in 20 minutes?

TH: Um… yes, that's fine. Do you have my number? It's…

TH: Tony Hopps speaking.

KM: Hello, Mr Hopps. It's Kelly Masterman here. I spoke to the ship's first officer. It seems that the porthole in your cabin was broken by the previous passenger and water was coming in. But he apologized for not explaining what the problem was to you. **I'm afraid we can't <u>refund</u> the** whole cost of the trip, but we can refund you the extra cost for the cabin that you didn't have.

TH: Hmm, that doesn't seem much. And my fancy-dress costume?

KM: On our website you can find a document for insurance claims. Send in the form and **we'll deal with that within a week.** But, as I said, **we are really very sorry for these difficulties.** So, **we would like to offer you a** 10 per cent discount the next time you book an Argonaut holiday **as compensation for** the problems you had. Is that acceptable to you, Mr Hopps?

TH: Well, er, yes, I think that sounds reasonable.

Understanding

Kelly Masterman took some notes during her phone call with Tony Hopps. Complete her notes.

Tony Hopps – Queen of the Waves

<u>Complaints:</u>

- *cabin problems:* ....
  ....
- *buffet lunch:* ....
  ....
- *programme changes:* ....
  ....
- *laundry:* ....
  ....

<u>Proposed action:</u>

- *refund:* ....
  ....
- *insurance claim:* ....
  ....
- *discount:* ....
  ....

Saying it accurately

1 **Match the two halves of the sentences, following the example.**

1. Could you bear with me for 10 minutes... → G
2. I'm terribly sorry for the...
3. I can imagine...
4. I propose that...
5. I'll make sure that it...
6. That must...
7. Could you tell me...
8. I do apologize...

A ...gets done by the end of the week.
B ...for our part in this.
C ...problems that you're experiencing.
D ...have been dreadful.
E ...we offer you some sort of compensation.
F ...exactly what happened?
G ...while I get to the bottom of what went wrong here?
H ...that was terrible.

2 **Put the sentences from *Saying it accurately 1* in the correct category, as shown in the example.**

To show regret/empathy
....
....
To find out what the problem is
1G
....
....
To apologize
....
....
To propose a solution/to promise action
....
....
....
....

3 **Read the telephone conversation again. Find more sentences to add to each of the categories in *Saying it accurately 2*.**

Saying it clearly

40

1 **Listen to these sentences, noting how the key words are stressed to make the speaker's meaning and intention clear.**

1. *I'm terribly sorry for the problems that you're experiencing.*
2. *I propose that we offer you some sort of compensation.*
3. *I'll make sure that it gets done by the end of the week.*
4. *I do apologize for our part in this.*

2 **Listen again to the sentences and repeat them.**

Saying it appropriately

41 **1** **Listen to two versions of this extract from a telephone call and answer the questions.**

Oh dear, I'm sorry to hear that. Let me just get a pen and I'll note them down. Right, can you give me the details?

1 Which version is more effective, the first or the second version?

2 Which words describe the most effective version?

A concerned

B distracted

C annoyed

D apologetic

E polite

F bored

42 **2** **Listen to the sentences from *Saying it accurately 1* and repeat them, copying the appropriate tone.**

Get speaking

43 **1** **Listen to four speakers making complaints. Respond to them, using expressions from *Saying it accurately 1* and *2*. Play the audio CD to start. When you hear the beep, pause and respond.**

44 **2** **You run a catering company, Simply Delicious Food. Your telephone is ringing and complaints are coming in. Play the audio CD to start. When you hear the beep, pause and respond.**

1 Express regret that there's a problem and find out exactly what the person is unhappy about.

2 Express empathy for the problem.

3 Summarize the problem for them.

4 Apologize for the problem and promise that you will take action on the points raised.

5 Propose a solution and check that this is acceptable for your client.

6 Propose a more substantial solution and check that this is acceptable.

7 Respond to the request and finish the call politely.

3 **Think about your workplace. What kinds of complaints do you deal with on a regular basis? How would you respond to them, using at least one phrase from this unit?**

9 Running a face-to-face meeting

So, let's get started.

USEFUL TIPS:

- Go through the agenda at the start of the meeting and check no items are missing.
- Ensure good timekeeping during the meeting, making sure that participants stick to the agenda and don't get sidetracked.
- Control the discussion, making sure all participants contribute where relevant and that no one person dominates the whole meeting.
- Summarize key decisions at the end of each agenda point.

Conversation

45

Janette is having a meeting with her team – Fabian, Lucy, and Tony – to discuss the rollout of a software program.

Janette: Everybody is here now. **So, let's get started.** Now, we're here to discuss the rollout of the new SAP customer relationship program. You are the people who'll have to implement it and we need to decide what you need for the rollout. **So, let's look at point number one on the agenda:** resources. **Fabian, would you like to start?**

Fabian: Right, at the moment there's a shortage of human resources to...

J: ...so by the time everyone has finished the training course, we should be OK. **So, to sum up point number one,** we've agreed that Lucy will arrange training sessions for the rollout team together with SAP and I'll talk to Human Resources about finding more SAP specialists.

Lucy: Thanks.

J: Good. **Let's move onto the next point:** budget. **Tony, that's your field.**

Tony: Well, I'm afraid that we have a very limited budget for this project, which means that we really have to be imaginative about how we allocate resources...

F: ...Does that mean training will be cut? Because look at the problems we had last year with the database. I spoke to Billy West in the data centre and he said that there was a problem with the —

J: **Can I stop you there,** Fabian? **Let's not get sidetracked.** Let Tony tell us what exactly is planned and then we can...

J: ...the meeting has been very useful. We all have our action points to deal with and we know the next steps. **How does everybody feel about that?**

T, L, and F: Fine. OK. Good.

J: Great! **So, that wraps up everything for today.** Thanks very much for all your ideas. Anybody want to go to lunch?

Understanding

Look again at the approaches outlined in *Useful tips*. Which tips does Janette follow? Underline the relevant parts of the dialogue and note the tips she uses in the margin. Which tip does Janette not follow?

Saying it accurately

1 **Complete the sentences with words from the box. Note that in some sentences, more than one word is possible.**

aim	welcome	down	make	started	start	fix	points
kick	sidetracked	begin	see	coming	sight	on	agree
point	thoughts	think	sum	agenda	agreed	up	look

Getting the meeting started

1 Thank you all for .... Let's get .... to business.
2 I'm glad you could all .... it. Perhaps we could make a ....
3 I'd like to .... you all here today. Let's get............. .

Setting out the aims of the meeting/going through the agenda

4 The .... of this meeting today is to .... next year's budget.
5 On the .... today are the following .... for discussion.
6 Looking at the agenda, you'll .... that there are five things to discuss today.

Introducing the first point for discussion

7 So, let's .... at .... number one.
8 John, would you like to .... ?
9 Lynn, would you like to .... things off?

Sticking to the agenda

10 Can you stop there, Paul? Let's not get ....
11 Let's not lose .... of the main objective here.
12 Shall we move .... to the next point?

Asking for contributions from others

13 Any .... on this, Janine?
14 Do we all .... on this?
15 What do you ...., Simon?

Summarizing and concluding

16 OK, that wraps .... everything for today.
17 So, let's just summarize the main things we've ....
18 So, to .... up, we've agreed the budget for next year.

46

2 Listen to the sentences to check your answers.

Saying it clearly

46

Listen to the sentences in *Saying it accurately 1* and repeat them.

Saying it appropriately

47

1 When we want to hear from other people at a meeting and to get their opinions, we use a rising intonation in the voice. Listen to these sentences and repeat them.

1 Any ideas about this, Ellen? ↗
2 Do we all think this is a good idea? ↗
3 Simon, what do you think? ↗
4 Is everyone happy with this, then? ↗
5 Shall we move on to the next point? ↗

48

2 To stop someone from digressing, interrupting, or dominating in a meeting, you need to be firm yet polite. Listen to these sentences and repeat them.

1 John, I think you're getting off the point here.
2 Paula, could we just hear what Neil has to say first?
3 Philippa, could we come back to your point in a moment?

Get speaking

1 You are chairing (managing) a meeting with Rita and Paolo to discuss the plans for the upcoming company conference. Here is your agenda.

Meeting to discuss upcoming company conference
Date: 3 March
Time: 10 a.m.
Attendees: You (chair), Rita Kay, Paolo di Franco

Agenda
Point one: Programme for the day
Point two: Possible locations

49

You start. Begin by chairing the meeting, covering the first three points. Then play the audio CD and follow the cues.

1 Get the meeting started.
2 Go through the agenda for the meeting.
3 Introduce the first point of discussion and ask Rita to contribute.
4 Say that you like Rita's suggestion and ask Paolo what he thinks.
5 Say that you like Paulo's suggestion and ask him to come up with some detailed suggestions on this.
6 Move the meeting onto point two on the agenda and ask Rita to contribute.
7 Get the meeting back on track and ask Rita to continue.
8 Say that you like Rita's idea and ask her to get some prices for you.
9 Summarize the main points of the meeting and the action items and check that they agree.
10 Check if they have anything else to add.
11 Conclude the meeting.

2 **Write an agenda for a meeting at your workplace. How would you start the meeting? Practise aloud and record yourself if possible, for review.**

Remember to sound:

- positive
- interested
- keen to hear what other people think.

Language note

Note the use of *so, right,* and *well* as signals in the meeting. When these kinds of words are said emphatically, they serve to direct the conversation.

***So**, let's get started.*
***Right**, at the moment...*
***Well**, I'm sure everybody...*

Cultural note

The scope of meetings varies from country to country. For example, in Japan, decisions are not usually made in a meeting between two companies. Rather, meetings are simply a way of exchanging information, which is then discussed internally before a decision is made. In the USA, however, if all the key members of staff are present, a decision may be made there and then. Similarly, etiquette for meetings varies considerably. For example, in Germany a degree of formality is required whereas in Spain, it is not unusual for attendees to speak over each other to get their point across.

10 Negotiating agreement

Well, that's an interesting proposal, but...

USEFUL TIPS: Successful negotiations usually follow this process:

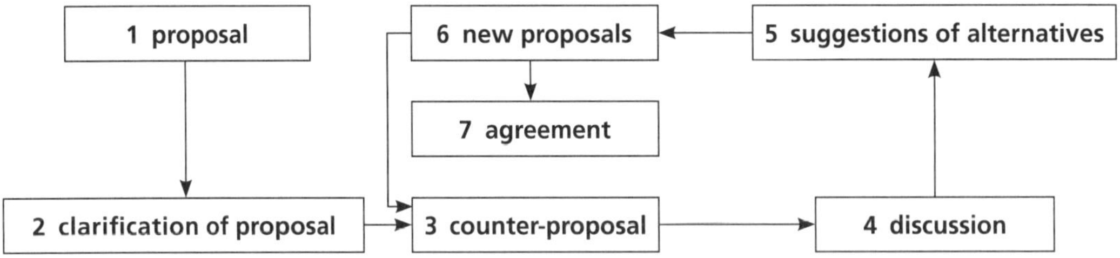

Conversation

50

Janette wants to hire some specialists from a consultancy company for a short-term project to roll out a software package worldwide for her company. She is meeting Stuart, a senior partner from the consultancy, to discuss fees for their services.

Janette: And that, basically, is why I called you, Stuart. We don't have enough SAP specialists for this job ourselves.

Stuart: I see. So, what exactly do you need?

J: **We propose that** you second us five programmers for customizing the basic SAP package to our needs, two web interface experts to make sure the package is user-friendly and one technical project manager.

S: OK. But **we need to talk about** fees. They would have quite different daily rates: €650 for a programmer, €875 for the interface specialists and, um, at least €1,250 for a project manager. Depending on his or her experience.

J: Well, we'd like to keep the bookkeeping easy. So, we'd like to aggregate these daily rates. **We suggest that** we pay you €700 per head per day.

S: I see. Well, **that's an interesting proposal, but** €700 per day is far too low. €950 is nearer the mark.

J: **I don't think we could go along with that**. You see, we have very strict budget limits.

S: Hmm... **Let's think about how we can make this work**... **Another possibility might be** to have two rates: €650 for the programmers and €950 for the others.

J: But **have you considered the advantages of** just one single flat rate? It makes the administration so much easier. I mean, **what's the downside?**

S: **I take your point.** It's just a question of agreeing the rate.

J: Right. So, by my calculations **if we agree on a daily rate of €750 per head per day, over six months your company will receive**... just a second... €772,000.

S: €750 per head per day for six months. Yes, I think we **can live with that.**

J: Excellent! So, now we just need to decide which people will be most suited...

Understanding

Look again at the stages of negotiation outlined in *Useful tips.* Write the stages in the correct place in the column on the left.

Stage	Sentences from the conversation
	Another possibility might be to have two rates: €650 for the programmers and €950 for the others. But have you considered the advantages of just one single flat rate?
	We need to talk about fees.
	Well, that's an interesting proposal, but €700 per day is far too low. €950 is nearer the mark.
	I take your point. We can live with that.
	We suggest that we pay you €700 per head per day.
	If we agree on a daily rate of €750 per head per day, over six months your company will receive €772,000.
	Another possibility might be to have two rates: €650 for the programmers and €950 for the others. But have you considered the advantages of just one single flat rate?
	Let's think about how we can make this work.

Saying it accurately

1 **Match the phrases and sentences on the left with those on the right that have similar meanings.**

1 We propose that…
2 We need to talk about…
3 I don't think we could go along with that.
4 Another possibility might be to…
5 I take your point.
6 We can live with that.

A I see where you're coming from.
B That's not going to work for us.
C Let's take a closer look at…
D We can go along with that.
E We suggest that…
F Instead, we could always do…

2 **Read the continuation of Janette and Stuart's negotiation and complete the sentences with expressions from *Saying it accurately 1.***

J: Of course, (1)... the subject of expenses. (2).................................. you cover the travel expenses for all the specialists during their stay.

S: Hmm, I'm afraid that (3)... .

J: OK, (4)... split the cost between us instead?

S: Well, OK, (5).. we pay 20 per cent and you pay 80 per cent.

J: No, sorry (6)... . How about we say 50–50 because, as we do most of our work locally, such costs are not built in to our fees.

S: Yes, I think (7)................................... .

J: Great!

Saying it clearly

51

1 **Listen to the following sentences, noting how the syllable stress changes when the word form changes.**

1 *We'll present our findings to the client.*
We'll be doing a presentation in the board room.

2 *We suggest that we increase the budget.*
That's a suggestion worth considering.

3 *Another possibility might be to hire more staff.*
Would it be possible to hire more staff?

4 *Have you considered the advantages of temporary staff?*
I'll certainly take that into consideration.

2 **Listen to the sentences again and repeat them.**

Saying it appropriately

1 **When negotiating, it is important to phrase your proposals politely and respectfully. Compare the following pairs of sentences.**

We recommend that you give us five programmers.
Give us five programmers.

We suggest the agreement is for a period of twelve months.
The agreement must be for a period of twelve months.

We want a 10 per cent discount.
We propose that you offer us a 10 per cent discount.

52 **2** **Listen to the sentences again and repeat the polite ones.**

53 **3** **When negotiating, you may want to make a positive comment on a proposal without committing yourself fully. Listen to these sentences and repeat them.**

1 Well, that's a proposal that's worth considering.
2 We'll certainly bear that in mind.
3 Well, that's something that we should discuss further.
4 Right, we're certainly open to the idea.

Get speaking

54 **1** **You are in a meeting to negotiate a deal with a building contractor to renovate your office. Listen to the audio CD to hear their quotation and then follow the cues. When you hear the beep, pause and respond.**

1 Ask the contractor to clarify exactly what that price will include.
2 Reject his proposal as it stands and put forward a counter-proposal of $150,000 including materials.
3 Reject his counter-proposal. Suggest $160,000 including materials. Point out the advantages of working for you because you plan to renovate all your offices around the country next year and so this project could lead to a lot more work for him in the future.

2 **Write a dialogue based on a negotiation from your work experience. Remember to include all stages of the process before reaching an agreement.**

Grammar note

Note how we use the first conditional to indicate that we are close to reaching agreement on a point.

Examples from the text:

If we agree on a daily rate of €750 per head per day over six months, your company *will* receive €772,000.

If we pay their travelling expenses, then they *won't [will not]* be out of pocket.

If he delivers the product by Friday, then *it'll [will]* be on the shelves by Monday.

The bank won't *[will not]* have any concerns *if we guarantee* the loan.

11 Assigning action points

Who would like to take responsibility for this?

USEFUL TIPS:

- Ask people to agree to action points rather than simply telling them to do something.
- For a general action point, e.g. organizing somebody to look after visitors to a company, offer the opportunity to anybody from the team. It may be seen as attractive, especially if it involves entertaining the visitors.
- If the action point is unattractive, such as writing the minutes of a meeting, and nobody volunteers, then ask the most qualified person. If necessary, ask if they can reprioritize other tasks.
- Summarize who is responsible for what and when they have agreed to deliver.

Conversation

55 **Janette is having a meeting with her team – Lucy, Fabian, and Tony – to discuss the rollout of a software program.**

Janette: …and we need to work together with SAP experts on this if we want to get the rollout to work properly, right?

Lucy, Fabian, and Tony: Yeah. Looks like it.

J: So, we need to speak to SAP about running a training program for all the system users. **Could you handle that,** Lucy?

L: Sure, I'll call Dieter Grossmann.

J: **How soon can you** finish the complete training program, **do you think?**

L: To train everybody, we'll need about three months. So, **not until** the end of September.

J: Great, now the project kick-off meeting. We all agreed to have it on the twentieth of July but nobody has done anything yet, have they? No, I thought not. I know I haven't! Well, we need to move fast on that, so Fabian, **could you deal with that?** Invitations to start with, refreshments, you know.

F: Of course.

J: **When will the invitations be ready, do you think?**

F: I'll do them this afternoon.

J: Fine. **I'd like to have them out by** this evening. Now, next week one of our biggest customers, Dimitri Mischkovic, is coming from Moscow to visit the company. He's arriving on Friday night and is staying here until Wednesday next week. Originally, I was going to take him out in London at the weekend, but my mother is in hospital. **So I need somebody to** take him out, all expenses paid by the company, of course. **Who would like to take responsibility for this?**

T: Oh, I don't mind. I mean, if nobody else wants to that is.

F: That's OK with me.

L: I don't think my boyfriend would like me going around London with somebody else anyway!

J: Good, I'll send you the details, Tony. Now, item number four on the agenda: we are going to be audited.

T, F and L: No. Not again! So soon?

J: Yes. Company policy, I'm afraid. I need somebody to write a report on our business activities over the last twelve months. **Is anybody interested in** doing that? Tony, **how do you feel about taking responsibility for that?** You have the most experience.

T: Well, it's a bit difficult, Janette, you know. I've got the department meeting to organize and then the budget to do and then Mr Mischkovic.

F: I could look after Mr Mischkovic for you, Tony.

T: No, I mean, I'm not saying I —

J: **Would you mind prioritizing this,** Tony? It's really very important.

T: Oh. Well, I suppose so.

J: Thanks. **Can you send me the report by Friday midday?** Then you can relax over the weekend with Mr Mischkovic!

Understanding

Make notes about the points agreed upon during the meeting.

Employee	Task(s) allocated	Finish date/time
Tony	• *Taking care of Dimtri Mischkovic during his stay*	*This weekend*
Lucy		
Fabian		

Saying it accurately

1 **Read these requests and decide in which category they belong. Follow the examples.**

- asking for volunteers to complete a task: *1*
- allocating a task to a particular person: *2*
- determining a completion time for the task: *3*

1 Would anyone like to put themselves forward for this?
2 Can I leave that with you, Jean?
3 Can you send me that by next Monday?
4 Could you take care of that, Kumiko?

5 How soon do you think you can finish that?
6 I'm looking for somebody to look after this.
7 Is anybody interested in doing this?
8 Could you deal with that?
9 Who would like to take responsibility for the minutes?
10 Is end February realistic as a deadline?
11 When will that be ready, do you think?
12 Could you handle that?
13 Will you be able to get that done by tomorrow?
14 Would you take responsibility for that, David?
15 Are there any volunteers to do this?

2 **Complete these requests with words from the box.**

of	by	for	about	with	in

1 Can you take care .... that?
2 Is anyone interested .... doing this?
3 Who would like to take responsibility .... this?
4 How do you feel .... doing this?
5 When do you think the report will be ready .... ?
6 Will you deal .... that for me?

3 **Complete the conversation with questions from *Saying it accurately 2*.**

Janette: OK, and we also need to decide who is going to prepare the financial statements that the auditors will need to see.
(1) ....?
Fabian, (2) ....?
Fabian: I suppose so.
J: Great, thanks. (3) ....?
F: Would first thing Monday morning be OK?
J: Perfect, so, moving on...

Saying it clearly

56

Listen to the requests in *Saying it accurately 1* and repeat them.

Note that in the *Yes/No* questions, the intonation goes up and in the *Who/How/When* questions, the intonation can go down.

Can you I leave that with you, Jean? ↗

How do you feel about taking responsibility for that? ↘

Remember to stress the key syllables and words.

***When** will that be **rea**dy, do you think?*

Saying it appropriately

57

1 **When making a request, it is important to sound polite. Listen to six sentences from *Saying it accurately 2* and decide if the requests are phrased politely or impolitely.**

1 Can you take care of that? impolitely politely
2 Is anyone interested in doing this? impolitely politely
3 Who would like to take responsibility for this? impolitely politely
4 How do you feel about doing this? impolitely politely
5 When do you think the report will be ready by? impolitely politely
6 Will you deal with that for me? impolitely politely

58

2 **Listen to the sentences, now phrased politely, and repeat them.**

Get speaking

1 **You are in a project team meeting with five colleagues. Ask your colleagues to do the following tasks. If possible, record yourself for review.**

Task	Person	Completion date/time
1 Write the proposal for a new project.	Jessica	By Friday
2 Source samples for the new company logo.	Chris	By the end of the month
3 Prepare a quotation for a potential new client, Millwood and Co.	Ayisha	By next Thursday
4 Write an advertisement to go in the paper for a new office manager.	Dan	By the end of the day
5 Organize the purchase and delivery of the new IT hardware.	Sophie	By November

2 **Think about your own workplace. Make notes of requests you typically make to colleagues. Then practise them aloud.**

12 Running a teleconference

Hi, this is Lee Ming here.

USEFUL TIPS:

- One person should take the role of the facilitator. The facilitator should lay out the ground rules for the meeting at the start and control the participants. Only the facilitator should interrupt another speaker. Otherwise, it can get very confusing.
- As with regular meetings, there should be a clear agenda, if possible with strict time limits for each item.
- The facilitator should ask people by name to contribute to specific topics. Each speaker should give their name before speaking.
- Clarity is essential in a teleconference, so native speakers should aim to speak clearly, for example minimizing the use of difficult idioms, and non-native speakers should ask if anything is unclear.
- The facilitator should do a summary of all points discussed at the end of the teleconference.

Conversation

59 **Janette is facilitating a telephone conference from London with participants from around the world, Petra, Carlo, Sanjay, and Lee Ming.**

Janette: …so that's Petra, Carlo, Sanjay. We're just waiting for Lee Ming and then –

System: *Ping*! Speaker five is entering the conference room.

Lee Ming: Hi, **this is Lee Ming here.**

J: Great! So, **it's Janette here.** Thank you all for participating today. Before we start, let's just check some ground rules for telephone conferences. **Please always give your name first,** so that we all know who's speaking. Also, **don't interrupt other speakers, please.** I'll make sure that we keep the conversation on track and don't lose any time. Finally, **please could you make sure that you speak clearly** and **just let me know if anything is unclear?** OK?

Petra, Carlo, Sanjay, and Lee Ming: Yes. Fine. Good. OK.

J: Right, let's run through the agenda. First of all we want to look at…

P: …the hardware and the software is now being tested and will be ready —

C: But Petra, that's not the problem at all! We need to know when!

J: Janette here. **Sorry Carlo, can you let Petra finish?** As I said at the beginning of the teleconference, just **one speaker at a time.**

C: Ah yes. Um, Carlo here. Sorry about that. **Could you repeat that, Petra?** About the software testing?

P: Petra here. No problem. So it'll be ready…

S: …and we think that the advantages of <u>outsourcing</u> all activities to Mumbai will be much greater if we are working closely with Singapore.

LM: Hmm. Lee Ming here. **I'm not sure what you mean by 'closely'.**

S: Sanjay here. Well, we have a lot of software programmers who could quickly develop the products that your people in Singapore design.

J: Janette here. **What do you think about that**, Lee Ming?

LM: Lee Ming here. Um, well it depends on what the designers are looking for because...

J: ...Well, that was all very helpful, I think. **So, let me recap our discussion.** The next step is for all of us to begin work on speaking with all the key suppliers in Mumbai...

...and when that's finished, the project will be over. **Is that acceptable to you,** Sanjay and Lee Ming?

S and LM: Yes. That's fine.

J: And **how about you,** Petra and Carlo? Any questions?

P and C: No, I'm happy. Sounds good.

J: Excellent! Then, I think that's enough for today. We have another meeting scheduled for...

Understanding

A secretary took some notes for the minutes. Complete her notes.

At the start Janette laid out ground rules. She asked speakers to:

- ....
- ....
- ....

.... *interrupted* .... *when she was talking about software testing.*

.... *asked* .... *to clarify what he meant by working 'closely' together.*

Everyone agreed on an action point to start discussions with ....

Another teleconference is booked.

Saying it accurately

1 **Put these sentences from the beginning of a teleconference in the correct order.**

[ ] Before we start, let's just lay out some ground rules for telephone conferences.
[ ] Finally, just let me know if anything is unclear.
[ ] Firstly, please always give your name first.
[*1*] So, it's Karen here.
[ ] Right, let's run through the agenda.
[ ] Secondly, don't interrupt other speakers, please.
[ ] Thank you all for participating today.
[ ] Thirdly, please could you make sure that you speak clearly?

2 **Complete the sentences with words from the box.**

finish	come	interrupt	sorry	speaker	finished	there	let

1 Excuse me, may I .... you there?
2 Sorry Hans, let Zara ....
3 Excuse me, I'm .... to interrupt, but...
4 One .... at a time, please.
5 Sorry, can I .... in here?
6 Sorry Kim, can I stop you .... ?
7 Fabrice, I don't think Chris has .... yet.
8 Gill, please could you .... Alex finish?

3 **Match the two halves of these questions used to ask for clarification and repetition.**

1 Sorry, but I don't... *B*
2 Sorry, but I didn't quite catch that. Could you...
3 Sorry, I'm afraid...
4 Excuse me, but I'm not sure...

A ...I missed that. Could you say it again, please?
B ...quite follow you. Could you repeat what you just said?
C ...what you meant by that. Would you mind repeating it?
D ...run that by me one more time?

Saying it clearly

60

1 **Listen to twelve sentences from *Saying it accurately 1, 2* and *3* and repeat them.**

Note how the speaker's intonation goes **down** when introducing a teleconference, interrupting politely and dealing with interruptions, but **up** when asking for clarification and repetition.

Before we start, let's just check some ground rules for telephone conferences. ↘

Fabrice, I don't think Chris has finished yet. ↘

Sorry, can I come in here? ↘

Excuse me, but I'm not sure what you meant by that. Would you mind repeating it? ↗

Saying it appropriately

61

1 **Listen to these four requests, deciding whether the speaker sounds polite or impolite.**

1	Please always say your name first.	impolite	polite
2	Begin by saying your name, please.	impolite	polite
3	Please don't cut in on people.	impolite	polite
4	Please don't interrupt other speakers.	impolite	polite

62

2 **Listen to the requests, this time said politely, and repeat them.**

Get speaking

1 **You are the facilitator at a meeting in Berlin with the following participants:**

Kazumi from Japan
Pierre from France
Emin from Turkey
Jake from the USA

Introduce yourself, welcome the participants, and lay out the ground rules for the teleconference.

63

2 **The meeting is underway. Play the audio CD to start. When you hear the beep, pause and respond. Use the prompts below to interrupt appropriately.**

1 Interrupt politely and deal with Emin interrupting Pierre.
2 Interrupt politely and ask Jake to clarify what he means and not to use idioms.
3 Interrupt politely and ask Pierre to repeat what he said.
4 Interrupt politely and ask Emin if he agrees with the suggestion.
5 Interrupt politely and remind speakers not to talk at the same time.

3 **Imagine that you are facilitating a teleconference for a project team at your workplace.**

First, make notes on:

- how you are going to start the meeting
- who is at the project team meeting
- the purpose of the meeting.

Then start the teleconference with an introduction to the meeting:

- introduce yourself
- welcome the participants
- lay out the ground rules
- go through the agenda.

13 Presenting a product or service

I want to tell you today about...

USEFUL TIPS: When presenting a product or service, an effective way to convince your audience is to follow the FAB approach:

- **Feature**: highlight the features of the product or service you want the audience to focus on.
- **Advantage**: show how these features make the product or service better than its predecessors or competitors.
- **Benefit**: show how this product or service will improve the user's life.

This approach can be grouped into a three-step presentation structure:

1 Introduction: summarize what you are going to tell the audience.
2 Main body: tell them.
3 Conclusion: tell them what they should do next.

Conversation

64

Steve Dunn, sales representative for Compix Inc, is presenting a new Customer Relationship Management (CRM) piece of software called iCustomer.

Steve: Well, **good afternoon, ladies and gentlemen.** I'm Steve Dunn **and I want to tell you today about** Compix's new CRM application for your iPhone, the iCustomer.

Firstly, I'll demonstrate exactly what this software is capable of doing.

Then, I'll outline the advantages this has over conventional CRM systems.

Finally, I'll show you how this can help boost the productivity of your salesforce significantly.

So, first of all, as a salesman I can tell you what we all want is up-to-the-minute information about our customers. iCustomer links your salespeople directly with your central customer database so that at any time they can check what exactly the...

...without any time lost. **Moving on to my next point, what are the advantages of** the real-time information provided by iCustomer over other CRM systems? Well, it means that for the first time ever your salespeople ***always*** have up-to-date details about your customers. Current credit ratings for example, any problems with recent orders or maybe a new special offer that headquarters wants...

...of course, because it has a phone function. **So, finally, what are the real benefits** for your salespeople? Two words: increased productivity. Our research shows that salespeople are able to make at least 15 per cent more customer visits per week, leading to an increased sales volume of up to 30 per cent and that's not all. With...

In conclusion, if you commit to using iCustomer, we are offering a free consultancy service for your business. Our experts will visit your company and...

Thank you for listening. **If anyone has any questions, I'd be happy to answer them**.

Customer: Yes, I do. Do you provide software training for users as part of the package?

Steve: **I'm pleased that you asked that question.** We don't provide training ourselves, but our sister company is responsible for that and I'm sure we could discuss ways that we could incorporate that into the package...

Understanding

64

Steve follows the FAB approach outlined in *Useful tips*. Listen again without reading and tick the *features*, *advantages*, and *benefits* of iCustomer that he mentions.

1 **Features**

A iCustomer allows your customers to place orders directly with the company.

B iCustomer provides a link between salespeople and customers' data.

C iCustomer provides a link between salespeople and suppliers.

2 **Advantages**

A Your salespeople always have current information about customers.

B It's cheap and easy to install.

C It's more user-friendly than any other system.

3 **Benefits**

A You will save money.

B You will produce a better product.

C Your salesforce will be able to sell more products.

Saying it accurately

1 **Steve goes on to present another new product, the Top-spy Anti-virus System 4 (TAS 4). Reorder the extracts from this presentation for a new security system so that it follows the FAB approach.**

1 By installing TAS 4, you will save time and money by protecting your computers against viruses.

2 It's well worth upgrading to TAS 4 because of its low RAM or memory usage compared to previous versions. Consumer surveys have also shown it to be more reliable than other systems currently available.

3 TAS 4 is a comprehensive Internet security system including a firewall and antispyware.

2 **Match Steve's phrases or sentences on the left with those on the right that serve the same purpose.**

1 I want to tell you today about...
2 Firstly, I'll demonstrate... Then, I'll outline... Lastly, I'll show you...
3 Moving onto my next point, ...
4 What are the advantages of...?
5 In conclusion,...
6 If anyone has any questions, I'd be happy to answer them.
7 I'm pleased you asked that question.

A First of all, I'll... Next, I'll... And finally, I'll...
B Let's look now at...
C My talk today is about...
D Please feel free to ask questions.
E To sum up,...
F That's a good question.
G Why is this important? Because...

3 **Complete Steve's presentation using phrases from *Saying it accurately 2.***

.... Telesmart, a new communications package we're offering to our loyal customers. .... demonstrate how it works. .... outline the advantages compared to other packages available .... show you how it can benefit your business...

...which means that you can combine all your business communications in one single package. .... Because it is much more straightforward than having a number of different providers for each service. .... how much money this can save you every year...

...and so, ..., Telesmart is a convenient way of saving you money. Thank you for your time. Now over to you. ....

Saying it clearly

65

1 **Listen to an extract of Steve's presentation in *Saying it accurately 1*.**

Note how Steve's intonation is varied, which makes the presentation interesting to listen to. He also emphasizes important words, such as product name and features, advantages, and benefits.

*TAS 4 is a **comprehensive Internet security system** including a **firewall** and **antispyware**.*

2 **Listen to Steve again. Repeat the sentences, using the same emphasis on key words. Pause when you need to.**

Saying it appropriately

66

1 **The way you deliver your presentation is almost as important as what you say. Listen to sentences from the presentation in *Saying it accurately 3*. Tick the statements that are true about the speaker's style of delivery.**

1 The presenter sounds confident and self-assured.
2 She sounds nervous and uncomfortable.
3 She sounds bored when talking about her product.
4 She sounds passionate when talking about her product.
5 The presentation is slow and boring.
6 The presentation is well-paced and easy to follow.
7 The presentation is rushed and hard to follow.

2 **Listen again to the presentation and repeat it.**

Get speaking

1 **Steve had to pull out of the presentation at the last minute and he gave you his notes about iCustomer and TAS 4. Deliver his presentation of the two products, using the notes below. Include phrases from the unit. If possible, record yourself for review. Compare your presentation to Steve's.**

Product	Features	Advantages	Benefits
iCustomer	It provides a link between salespeople and customers' data.	Your salespeople always have up-to-date information about customers.	Increased productivity: salespeople can make 15 per cent more customer visits per week and 30 per cent more sales.
TAS 4	A comprehensive Internet security system including firewall and antispyware.	• low RAM compared to previous versions. • consumer survey showed it to be more reliable than other systems available.	You will save time and money by protecting computers from viruses.

2 **Complete this table with the features, advantages, and benefits of a product or service from your line of work. Then deliver your presentation. If possible, record it for review.**

Product/service	Features	Advantages	Benefits

14 Working on a stand

Would you be interested in finding out more about this?

USEFUL TIPS: When working on a stand, ask questions rather than simply presenting products. This will give the stand visitor the feeling that the focus is on their interests and needs.

- Find out what business the visitor is in and who their customers are.
- Find out what their customers want.
- Find out what would make the visitor's life easier and suggest ways to help them achieve that goal.

Conversation

67

Amanda is a salesperson for Compix Inc, a software development company. She is on the stand at a computer industry trade fair in Los Angeles.

Amanda: Hi there. **Can I help you?**

Colin: What? Oh me? I was just looking at some of these brochures.

A: Well, I'm Amanda.

C: Ah. I'm Colin.

A: **What field of business are you in**, Colin?

C: I'm a specialist publisher. I don't really know much about computer software and hardware, I'm afraid. I publish books about stamp collecting.

A: **Really? Who are your customers?**

C: Well, different types of people. Children, teenagers, adults, people who have retired... mostly male, of course.

A: I see. **And what are your customers looking for?**

C: Well, information and books about stamps. Particularly prices, trade fairs or articles about the history of particular stamps.

A: OK... but **what are the challenges you face in** reaching them?

C: Well, there are lots of stamp collectors, but they're all over the world. It's very hard to reach them so it's difficult to sell my company's books. Normal bookshops won't take them. So I put advertisements in stamp magazines, but that's expensive.

A: Of course. Well, **would you be interested in something to** help you reach a worldwide audience, 24/7?

C: Using the Internet, I suppose I would. But I don't know anything about programming.

A: Ah, but **what would you think about** a tool that does that for you? A tool that lets you just upload the documents that you want into a template? And one that also saves information about customers so you can...

C: ...but that's really very interesting. So you think that a free newsletter would help my business?

A: Definitely. At Compix, we have one that we send to our customers every quarter with information about new developments in the industry. In fact, **can I add you to our mailing list?**

C: Hmmm, well yes, of course.

A: Great! **Can you give me your card?** Then I have all your details and I'll make sure that you are kept up to date on what we're doing...

C: That sounds great. Can I take one of these demo software packages?

A: **Unfortunately, I'm afraid** I can't give you one today. **I'm so sorry** about that. But I can send you one.

C: OK. That's better. That way I don't have to carry it around with me all day.

Understanding

Amanda made some notes following her conversation with her potential customer, Colin. Complete her notes with the missing information.

Name:	*Colin*
Field of business:	
Customers:	
Customers looking for:	
Challenges:	
Add to mailing list?	Yes/No
To do:	

Saying it accurately

1 **Using the prompts, make questions to find out more about a potential customer.**

1 What / line of work / in? ....

2 What / involve / exactly? ....

3 What sort / customers / have? ....

4 What / your customers / want? ....

5 What / help you / help your customers? ....

6 What / issues / face in your line of work? ....

2 **Match the questions in *Saying it accurately 1* to the following answers.**

A Competition and rising food prices are our main challenges.

B I own a small catering business.

C It would help if we could set up a better way of communicating with our customers so that we can make sure that they are satisfied and use their feedback to improve our performance.

D Mostly large companies.

E They want us to supply a high quality product for a fair price.

F We supply food and drink to conference venues around the country.

3 **Kay works in marketing and is having a meeting with a potential customer, Jon. Number the sections of the conversation in the right order, 1–15.**

[ ] **Kay:** Well, would you be interested in hearing more about our website design service to publicize what you do?

[ ] **Kay:** Hello Jon, nice to meet you. First of all, what line of work are you in?

[ ] **Kay:** And what does that involve exactly?

[ ] **Jon:** I'm a surveyor.

[ ] **Kay:** What sort of customers do you have?

[ ] **Jon:** Yes, I would.

[ ] **Kay:** Here's some more information on that then. And can I add you to our mailing list?

[ ] **Jon:** Well, I carry out valuations and building surveys on properties for clients.

[ ] **Jon:** That sounds like a good idea. I think it would be useful to keep up-to-date with any new marketing ideas.

[ ] **Kay:** What challenges do you face in your line of work?

[ ] **Kay:** And what do your customers want from you?

[*1*] **Jon:** Hello Kay, I'm Jon.

[ ] **Jon:** We find it hard to get our message out to new clients without spending lots of money on advertising.

[ ] **Jon:** Mainly small businesses or private purchasers.

[ ] **Jon:** They are looking for a professional service that is delivered promptly and is good value for money.

68 **4** **Listen to the conversation to check your answers.**

Saying it clearly

69 **1** **Listen to the questions from *Saying it accurately 1 and 3*.**

Remember how the questions that have a *Yes/No answer* go up and questions that *start with wh- words* can go down.

What sort of customers do you have? ↘

Would you like me to show you our new product? ↗

69 **2** **Listen again to the questions from *Saying it accurately* 1 and 3 and repeat them.**

Grammar note

When forming questions, invert the subject and the auxiliary verb.

Examples from the text:

Can I help you with anything in particular? What field of business *are you* in?

Would you like me to show you a tool that does that for you?

Saying it appropriately

70 **1** **Listen to three people on a stand who are trying to generate interest in a new product. Match the speakers to the descriptions.**

speaker 1	**A** pushy and aggressive
speaker 2	**B** assertive and excited about their product
speaker 3	**C** shy and bored

70 **2** **Which speaker is likely to generate the most interest in the product and why? Listen again to this speaker and repeat what is said.**

3 **Sometimes on a stand, you cannot do what a customer would like.**

C: Can I take one of these demo software packages?

A: ***Unfortunately, I'm afraid*** *I can't give you one.* ***I'm sorry*** *about that.*

When you apologize, it is important to use the right phrase *and* to sound apologetic. Listen to these apologies and write in the missing words.

1 I'm .... sorry but I haven't got any brochures left.
2 Unfortunately, I forgot to bring my business cards. I do ....
3 I'm .... I can't help on you on this. I'll ask a colleague.

71 **4** **Listen to the apologies on the audio CD and repeat them. Make sure you really do sound apologetic.**

Get speaking

72 **You work for a technology company on a stand at a trade fair. Start a conversation with a potential customer. Play the audio CD and follow the cues. You start with the first question.**

1 Ask him if you can help.
2 Ask him what line of work he is in.
3 Ask him who his customers are.
4 Ask him what his customers want.
5 Ask him what challenges he faces.
6 Ask him if he would be interested in hearing about a new video link teleconferencing system that would allow him to have meetings with customers around the world.

15 Closing a sale

We only have this offer for a short time.

USEFUL TIPS: When closing a sale, frame the sales pitch as an open question so that, if the customer has any questions or objections, it is still possible for the salesperson to respond. Once the request has been made, be quiet and let the customer decide!

These are three possible styles for closing a sale:

- Hard close: assume that the customer wants to buy the product/service and ask for quantities or delivery dates.
- Emotional close: point out to the customer the advantages of having the product or the disadvantages of not having it and appeal to their emotions.
- Urgent close: tell the customer that the product is only available for a short time due to scarcity, or that the price will soon rise.

Conversations

73

Amanda and Steve from Compix Inc are talking to four different customers at a computer industry trade fair in Los Angeles about a new gadget from their company, a hand-held product scanner.

1

Amanda: ...really does the job, so with our PriceChex product scanner, you just scan the price tag of any product in a shop and it does an automatic Internet search and tells you if the price in the shop is fair. But that's not all. It can also tell you where you can buy it cheaper! And it only costs $49.99!

Customer: Wow! That is so cool! But I want to have a look around at the other stands first and then —

A: Sure. I understand. But I should tell you, **we only have** ten of these items here at the trade fair...

C: Ah, um, I see. And how much did you say it cost?

2

Steve: ...software performs an automatic Internet search and tells you if the price in the shop is fair. But that's not all. It can also tell you where you can buy it cheaper! And it only costs $49.99!

C: That could be very useful for my team.

S: Definitely. So, **how many can I put you down for?**

C: Um, I'm not quite sure. Well, I think I'll take two for now and try them out with...

3

A: ...But that's not all. It can also tell you where you can buy it cheaper! And it only costs $49.99!

C: Really? My brother is always driving me crazy telling me how I paid too much for something.

A: Sounds like my mother-in-law. Just think. **What will you feel like when** you can scan something he's bought and then tell him he could have got it 50 per cent cheaper somewhere else?

C: That would be awesome! OK, I'll take two and I'll give him one for his birthday...

4

S: ...It can also tell you where you can buy it cheaper! And it only costs $49.99!

C: I see. I need to think about it. I'll come back tomorrow.

S: No problem. Only I wouldn't want you to be disappointed. The PriceChex **is only available at this price today! It's a special promotion for** the trade fair opening...

C: Oh dear! Well, could I reserve one and come back in a few minutes?

Understanding

Which style of close – hard, emotional, or urgent – is being used by the seller in each conversation?

conversation 1: ....

conversation 2: ....

conversation 3: ....

conversation 4: ....

Saying it accurately

1 Unscramble these words to make sentences that you could use when closing a deal.

1 it's / do / installed / you / How / think / look / will / it / when

.... ?

2 put / many / you / can / for / down / How / I

.... ?

3 available / today / at / only / It's / this / price

....

4 start / Shall / paperwork / we / the

.... ?

5 offer / time / for / have / only / this / short / a / We

....

6 six / stock / only / this / left / in / item / We've / got / of

....

7 see / What / people / it / say / will / when / they

.... ?

8 in / you / it's / What / feel / when / will / like / place

.... ?

9 start / you / When / like / would / to

.... ?

2 **Look again at the sentences from *Saying it accurately 1* and decide in which category they belong. Follow the example.**

a hard close:	
an emotional close:	*1*
an urgent close:	

Saying it clearly

74

1 **Listen to these three sentences and read the following notes.**

Hard close: *How many can I put you down for?*

Emotional close: *What will you **feel** like when you can see it in place?*

Urgent close: *It's **only** available at this price **today**.*

Note also how the speakers stress the emotional and urgent words in their sentences to reinforce their style of close.

2 **Listen again to the sentences in *Saying it clearly 1* and repeat them, using the same stress and intonation.**

Saying it appropriately

75

1 **Listen to the following sentences from *Saying it accurately 1*.**

Note how the speaker uses a *determined, business-like tone* of voice to make a **hard close**.

Note how the speaker sounds *friendly* when *empathizing* with the listener during an **emotional close**.

Note how the *urgency* can be detected in the speaker's tone of voice when they are making an **urgent close**.

2 **Listen again to the sentences from *Saying it accurately 1* and repeat them, using the same tone.**

3 **What mistakes do these sellers make? What should they have said instead, to stand a better chance of closing the deal? See *Useful tips* for hints.**

1 Seller: It's a great opportunity. Do you want it, yes or no?

Customer: No.

Seller's mistake: ....

Seller should have said: ....

2 Seller: Would you like to take the offer now, or do you want to think about it?

Customer: I'll have a think about it and get back to you.

Seller's mistake: ....

Seller should have said: ....

3 Seller: How many can I put you down for? It really is a great opportunity. And not one that comes along very often. In fact, I can't remember when we offered a better price on this. And we've been inundated with requests. Very high level of demand, which means that there might not be much stock left. And so it would be good if you could –

Customer: Sorry, I'm late for my next appointment. I'll get back to you.

Seller's mistake: ....

Seller should have said: ....

Get speaking

Practise closing sales using the strategies outlined below. Follow the example.

Example: *1. We have a special offer on this. The 24-hour call-out feature is included in the basic package at no additional cost. But we only have this offer for a short time.*

Product/service	Price/features	Closing style
1 IT support service	There is a special offer for limited time only. A 24-hour call-out feature is included in basic package at no additional cost.	urgent
2 Catering for company conference	The price is £8.99 per head for a full buffet.	hard
3 New office furniture	€10,000 will cover the supply of handmade Swedish desks and chairs throughout the office.	emotional
4 Audit of company accounts	$10,000 will cover the entire job.	hard
5 Cars for employees	The price is $5,000 per unit when you order more than twenty vehicles. Only fifty vehicles are left, otherwise you'll have to wait three months for next shipment.	urgent
6 Gym membership for employees	Corporate membership will cost only £30 per month and will be very popular with employees.	emotional

16 Saying 'no' politely

Thanks, but I have to say 'no'.

USEFUL TIPS: Saying 'no' is difficult for many people. It is, however, quite possible to say no without causing offence by adopting these strategies:

- Include an apology and, if possible, a brief explanation.
- Suggest that saying no is not your personal wish but is imposed by outside circumstances, for example, regulations or another appointment.
- Use emphasizers such as ***really***, ***so***, and ***very*** with the word *sorry*.

Conversations

76

Amanda and Steve from Compix Inc are talking to different customers at a computer industry trade fair in Los Angeles.

1

Steve: ...an automatic Internet search and tells you if the price in the shop is fair. But that's not all. It can also tell you where you can buy a product cheaper! And it only costs $49.99!

Customer 1: That could be useful for my team.

S: Definitely. So, would you like to make an order straight away?

C1: **I'd rather not, thank you.** Although it *is* a nice piece of software.

S: Exactly! Now, what if I gave you one to take away for yourself and then if you like it you can keep that one but order ten more for your team.

C1: **I'm really sorry, but that's not possible.** Company policy doesn't allow me to make that kind of deal.

S: I see. But let me just show you a couple of extra features that are *so* cool!

C1: **No, I'm sorry,** I have an appointment in ten minutes. **I don't really have the time right now.**

S: But you really need to see the way this program can slice and dice any information that—

C1: **Thanks, but I have to say no.** Ah, Terry, there you are, shall we go for that meeting? I was beginning to think that...

2

Amanda: ...an automatic Internet search and tells you if the price in the shop is fair. But that's not all. It can also tell you where you can buy a product cheaper! And it only costs $49.99!

Customer 2: `Well, that is interesting. I work for a computer magazine, which specializes in comparing different products.

A: Well, that's perfect! And as a journalist we can give you a special discount price if you order three licences. You only need to pay $125!

C2: **Unfortunately, that's just not possible.** I'm a freelance journalist so I really don't need three licences.

A: I understand. But maybe if you wrote a friendly article about us, you could have one licence for nothing.

C2: **Sorry, but that's out of the question.** I'd lose my job! We have to keep our independence from the computer industry.

A: I see. But would it be possible for me to visit your company later this month and maybe I could do a presentation for you and your colleagues?

C2: Well, thanks, **I'll get back to you on that one**. I must go now, but I have your card so I could give you a ring next week, if you like. Now I have to...

Understanding

Look again at the strategies outlined in *Useful tips*. Which strategies do the customers employ when saying no politely? Underline the relevant parts in the conversations and note the strategies used in the margin.

Saying it accurately

1 **Complete the sentences with words from the box.**

rather no back sorry possible not time thanks work question

1 No, I'm ....
2 Unfortunately that's just not ....
3 I'm really sorry, but that's not going to ....
4 I'm afraid ....
5 I'd .... not, thank you.
6 Thanks, but I have to say ....
7 I'm afraid I don't really have the .... right now.
8 Thanks, I'll get .... to you on that one.
9 Thanks, but no ....
10 Sorry, but that's out of the ....

2 **Drewery is trying to sell Jess some office equipment. Complete the conversation using sentences or phrases from *Saying it accurately 1*. Note that in some places, more than one answer is possible.**

Drewery: And so you can see what a great offer it is. Shall we sit down and discuss figures?

Jess: (1)................................... .

D: I could look at knocking down the unit price if you put in a large order?

J: (2)................................... because my manager has to place large orders.

D: Well then, perhaps you could just order a few samples?

J: (3)................................... because I'm meeting a colleague at 1 p.m.

D: I won't keep you a minute. Just have another quick look. These monitors really are state of the art. And, I tell you what, if you order just five, I'll throw in an extra free.

J: (4).. I'll give you a ring if we decide to proceed. Goodbye.

Saying it clearly

77 **1 Listen to different ways of saying no from *Saying it accurately 1*.**

Note how the speakers use a firm tone and how their voices go *down* to indicate their rejection of the proposal.

2 Listen again to the ways of saying no from *Saying it accurately 1* and repeat them.

78 **3 Listen to these sentences, noting how the sounds between words are connected. When one word ends with a consonant and the next starts with a vowel, the sounds are linked.**

*Sorry, but that'**s out of** the question.*

*Thanks, bu**t I** have to say no.*

*I'**m** afrai**d I** don't really have time.*

4 Listen to the three sentences again and repeat them.

Saying it appropriately

1 Jean is trying to say no to John politely. Choose the most appropriate response in each case.

1 John: So, shall I put you down for 100 units?

A Jean: No.

B Jean: Thanks, but I have to say no.

2 John: Are you sure? This offer is only valid until the end of the day?

A Jean: I'm afraid I can't make any orders without my boss's authorization.

B Jean: No, I don't want them.

3 John: I could even throw in free delivery.

A Jean: Not interested.

B Jean: I'm really sorry, but that's not going to work.

4 John: Oh, come on... This isn't an offer that comes along every day.

A Jean: I'm sorry, but it's out of the question.

B Jean: Look, I've already said no, haven't I?

79 **2 When saying no politely, you need to sound sincere. Listen to the following speakers and decide who is using an appropriate tone.**

speaker 1	sincere	insincere
speaker 2	sincere	insincere
speaker 3	sincere	insincere
speaker 4	sincere	insincere
speaker 5	sincere	insincere

80 **3 Listen to the sentences, this time said in an appropriate tone, and repeat them.**

Get speaking

81 **1 You are speaking to a sales representative at a trade fair. Play the audio CD to start. When you hear the beep, pause and respond suitably.**

1 Say no politely and explain that you don't have the budget to purchase additional software this year.

2 Say no politely and explain that you can't change company budgeting policy.

3 Say no strongly but politely and say goodbye.

82 **2 You are speaking to another sales representative. Play the audio CD to start. When you hear the beep, pause and respond, saying say no politely to all her suggestions. Try to use all three strategies outlined in *Useful tips*.**

Cultural note

Saying no comes more easily to business people in some cultures than in others, for example in Northern Europe where people tend to be direct. To some ears though, this directness may sound rude.

In contrast, in some countries people rarely say no, so a 'maybe' is commonly interpreted as a no. Elsewhere in the world though, a 'maybe' constitutes a real possibility of a 'yes'. This can lead to a breakdown in communications between business partners and waste a lot of time unnecessarily.

So, always try to be clear about your intentions, but remain polite at all times.

17 The successful job interviewer

What makes you suitable for this job, do you think?

USEFUL TIPS: When interviewing for a job, there are four main areas to ask about:

- work history
- personality
- suitability for the company and the specific job
- goals and ambitions.

Note that it is not appropriate to ask the candidate questions about race, age, marital status, or sexual preferences. These questions are potentially discriminatory.

Conversation

83

Mansha Khan is attending an interview for a sales position.

Chris H: …and so your online résumé was very interesting and that's why we asked you to come for an interview. I'm responsible for all human resources issues here at Bergerbild and my colleague here, Georgina Harris, is head of the sales department, which is where we currently have a position free.

Georgina H: Hello, nice to meet you.

Mansha K: Hi, nice to meet you too.

CH: Fine. So Mr Khan, **what do you know about our company**?

MK: A lot! You're involved in big overseas infrastructure projects in South-East Asia, for example, and among other things you are currently bidding for…

CH: …and the Kuching metro project was very successful. But coming back to you, Mr Khan, **what do you feel has been your biggest achievement to date?**

MK: Well, I introduced a new process for prioritizing customer visiting schedules for our department and in six months, we managed to increase sales by about 22 per cent. My manager was very pleased!

CH: Hmm, I can understand why. So, **why would you like to leave your current job?**

MK: Well, the sales position that you are offering would give me opportunities to work internationally. At the moment I'm just based in Seattle.

GH: I see. But **what makes you suitable for this job, do you think?**

MK: I've been very successful so far in sales and I think that I can offer a good service to your customers.

CH: Interesting point. **What is good customer service, in your view?**

MK: Definitely the most important skill is the ability to listen to what…

…but of course learning is a never-ending process for anybody in business.

GH: Very true. Now, **what are your weaknesses, would you say?**

MK: Well, my mom criticizes my untidiness around the house, but I guess you don't mean that. Hmm, I suppose I'm not very good at making sure all the paperwork involved in sales is completed quickly. You know, I prefer to be out there, going on to the next customer. But of course, I know it has to be done. I'm trying to improve.

GH: Well, you are quite young, aren't you?

MK: I'm 26.

CH: Right. Now, **what are your goals for the next five years?**

MK: I hope that I can also take on responsibility for organizing other salespeople in the future. I see myself in a management position when I have more experience and can share that experience with other salespeople.

GH: OK. Now, **what are your salary expectations?** For this sales position, I mean?

MK: Well, I'm sure that a mixture of...

Understanding

1 **Look again at the four interview areas outlined in *Useful tips*. Write them alongside the corresponding questions from the interview.**

- work history
- personality
- suitability for company and role
- goals and ambitions

To find out about the candidate's:	Questions from dialogue
	• What are your weaknesses, would you say?
	• What are your goals for the next five years?
	• What do you feel has been your biggest achievement to date? • Why would you like to leave your current job?
	• What do you know about our company? • What makes you suitable for this job, do you think? • What is good customer service, in your view?

2 **The interviewers say one potentially inappropriate thing. What is it?**

Saying it accurately

1 **Complete the sentences with a word from the box.**

challenges	**rewarding**	**see**	**hire**	**current**
yourself	**independently**	**situation**	**greatest**	**right**

1 Why should I .... you for this job?

2 Do you prefer to work .... or as part of a team?

3 Tell me a bit about ....

4 Tell me about a .... where you worked well under pressure.

5 What are your .... strengths and weaknesses?

6 What has been most .... about your current job?

7 What major .... have you faced in your current role? How have you handled them?

8 What's your .... salary?

9 Where do you .... yourself in five years?

10 Why do you think that you're .... for this job?

2 **Complete the conversation with questions from *Understanding 1* and *Saying it accurately 1*. In places, more than one answer may be correct.**

Mary: (1) ....?

Yiannis: Well, I think that I'd be suitable for the position because I've had lots of relevant experience in my previous roles. Also, I think I'd be a good fit for the company.

M: (2) ....?

Y: Quite a bit. I know that it's the second largest advertising company in the country and that you employ over 500 staff.

M: That's right. Now, tell me a bit about yourself. (3) ....?

Y: Hmm, interesting question. Well, I'm very hard-working and incredibly creative, as you can see from my portfolio. But, on the downside, I'm also a bit of a perfectionist, so I find it hard to let go of a project sometimes. But I'm working on that!

M: OK. And (4) ....?

Y: That would have to be when an advertisement that my team developed was nominated for Best Local Ad of the Year. It was great to get some acknowledgement for all our hard work.

M: Uh-huh. (5) ....?

Y: Well, I've enjoyed working for a small company and learned a lot, but I'd really like the opportunities that are offered by working for a large company, for example, the chance to pitch to big clients.

M: Right, so (6) ....?

Y: I'd like to be working as a senior advertising executive with a number of great campaigns under my belt.

84 **3** **Listen to the conversation from *Saying it accurately 2* to check your answers. Remember that in places, more than one answer may be correct.**

Saying it clearly

85

1 **Listen to these questions, noting how the underlined syllables are stressed.**

1. *What are your greatest strengths and weaknesses?*
2. *Why would you like to leave your current job?*
3. *Why do you think that you're right for this job?*
4. *What are your goals for the next five years?*

2 **Listen again to the questions in *Saying it clearly 1* and repeat them.**

Saying it appropriately

1 **It is very important that you only ask questions that are appropriate and professional. Tick the questions that would be appropriate in an interview.**

1. Tell me about your typical working day.
2. What's your star sign?
3. Do you go to church?
4. What is your greatest weakness?
5. Are you single?
6. Are you older than 40?
7. How would your friends describe you?
8. Are you a Hindu?
9. Do you come from China originally?
10. What's your greatest achievement to date?

86

2 **Listen to the seven interview questions from *Understanding 1* and repeat them, copying the speaker's interested and enthusiastic tone.**

Get speaking

87

You are interviewing someone for the position of assistant. Play the audio CD and follow the cues. You start.

1. Welcome the candidate and ask him about his suitability for this position.
2. Respond in an encouraging manner and then ask about his strengths and weaknesses.
3. Respond in an encouraging manner and ask him to give you an example of when he multitasked in his current job.
4. Respond in an encouraging manner and ask him about his reasons for leaving his current role.
5. Respond in an encouraging manner and ask him about his goals and ambitions for the next five years.
6. Respond in an encouraging manner and end the interview.

Would you consider employing this person for the job? Why/Why not?

18 The successful interview candidate

So, tell me about yourself.

USEFUL TIPS:

- Answer questions fully. Avoid very short answers.
- Be sure about the details on your résumé, and be prepared to talk about your achievements and experience in depth.
- Research the background of the company or organization.
- Listen carefully to the questions you are asked. Answer them with relevant information.

Interviews

88 **Karl Everett from Bergerbild is interviewing people for different positions in the European sales team.**

1

Karl: **I see from your résumé** that you have web design experience as well as in sales.

Candidate 1: Yes, that's right.

K: Hmm. That could be interesting for the development of our Internet presence in Europe. Our website is very US-oriented at the moment.

C1: Well, it's something I really enjoy doing. In my current job I was part of a team that did a redesign of the company website and I learned a lot.

K: What software can you work with?

C1: Well, I can use Dreamweaver, which is the classic web design tool of course, but I've also got experience of using...

2

K: So, **do you think you can make a useful contribution** to this company?

Candidate 2: Oh, yes.

K: I see.

C2: Yes.

K: Is your previous experience suitable for this position?

C2: Hmm. Yes. Yes, definitely.

K: And you don't think it would be difficult moving into a management position?

C2: No, I don't think so.

K: Really?

C2: No, not at all.

K: Right.

3

K: Perhaps you could tell me, **what do you know about this company?**

Candidate 3: Well, I know you have been very active in India over the last five years with the Mumbai City Transit System. What was it now? A two billion-dollar contract to provide not only the trains but also all the electronic equipment for the system, I think.

K: Yes, quite a difficult project. We had a lot of trouble with subcontractors.

C3: Yes, I understand it was very challenging. But in the end the project was completed on time and within budget. So you must have been pleased with the final result.

K: That's true and, of course, it is an excellent reference project for us...

4

K: Now, could you tell me, **what are your greatest strengths and weaknesses,** in your opinion?

Candidate 4: Hmm, that's an interesting question. Well, I think my greatest strength is that I never give up. In my experience, in order to win a customer you just have to really go on and on looking for a way to give them what they want and then you get the sale.

K: True. And what about weaknesses?

C4: Well, I need to improve my team player skills. Like many salespeople I don't like sharing customer information with other salespeople, but sometimes it makes the customer angry when he or she gets a visit from two different salespeople with different products from the same company. So, I realize it's necessary to share information, but it isn't easy for me to put this into practice.

K: Right. Well, here at Bergerbild, teamwork is very important.

C4: Yes, yes, I agree. I'm just telling you what I think is my greatest weakness. And I'm working on it.

5

K: So, perhaps you could tell me, **what has been your biggest achievement to date?**

Candidate 5: Oh well, I took part in this quiz competition a few years ago when I was at university. I was the head of the team and we got to the final of the national tournament. And we only just missed out on the top prize. So, there we were in the final round and the other team came from Cambridge —

K: Sorry, I meant more in the way of —

C5: and we both had eighteen points each and the question came up 'What are the main tributaries of the Volga?' Now I knew that.

K: I meant what was your biggest achievement at work?

C5: Oh, sorry, yes. Um, well, in my current job we have a team which takes part in quiz competitions in pubs and last year we got to the finals. There we were, facing a team from a pub in Cambridge when...

Understanding

Answer these questions about the five candidates.

Candidate	Would you hire this candidate?	Why/Why not?
1		
2		
3		
4		
5		

Saying it accurately

1 **Match the interview questions with the appropriate strategies to answer them.**

1 So, could you tell me about yourself?
2 Why do you want this job?
3 How would your colleagues describe you?
4 How do you cope with working under pressure?
5 What is your greatest strength?
6 What's your greatest weakness?
7 Are you a team player?
8 Where do you see yourself in five years' time?

A Always answer this question with a 'yes' and back it up with examples of times where you have demonstrated your ability to work as part of a team.
B Answer by emphasizing the positive aspects of your character that other people may have noticed.
C Answer to show that you are ambitious but not overly ambitious. Make sure that your answer implies that you envisage that you will still be working for the target company five years from now.
D Answer with care. If you say you have no weaknesses, then you are clearly lying. But, don't choose anything too serious that will make the interviewer lose interest in you. Instead, mention a small weakness, relevant to your work, which you are trying to improve.
E Don't give your life story. Simply give relevant facts relating to your education and work experience.
F Explain how the target position relates to your own experience, personality, and goals.
G Make sure that you choose a strength that is relevant to a work situation.
H Emphasize the positive aspects of your character that might emerge in a pressurized situation.

2 **Tick the words you might use to describe your strengths during an interview.**

consc<u>ien</u>tious
creative
dependable
determined
diplomatic
enthusiastic
experienced
fair
logical
loyal
methodical
motivated
practical
reliable
resourceful
trustworthy

Saying it clearly

89 **1** **Listen to the adjectives from *Saying it accurately 2*. Underline the syllable stress, following the example.**

2 **Listen again to the adjectives from *Saying it accurately 2* and repeat them.**

Saying it appropriately

90 **Listen to the audio CD. Decide in each case which candidate gives the most appropriate response to the question.**

question 1	candidate 1	candidate 2
question 2	candidate 1	candidate 2
question 3	candidate 1	candidate 2
question 4	candidate 1	candidate 2
question 5	candidate 1	candidate 2
question 6	candidate 1	candidate 2
question 7	candidate 1	candidate 2
question 8	candidate 1	candidate 2

Get speaking

91 **1** **Think of your own line of work and the kind of interview you might attend. Play the audio CD to start. When you hear the beep, pause and respond suitably.**

2 **Write another five questions you might be asked at an interview. Then practise answering them. Record yourself for review, if possible.**

Cultural note

There are non-verbal ways of making a good impression in an interview. Always dress appropriately. In most lines of business, conservative dress is the safest option. Remember to use appropriate body language. Greet your interviewers with a smile and a firm handshake (where appropriate) and, if you're being interviewed by a panel of people, try to make eye contact with all of them as you answer the questions.

19 Carrying out performance reviews

How do you feel about your performance this year?

USEFUL TIPS: The purpose of the performance review is for the line manager to review what the employee does, evaluate how well they perform, and discuss objectives for the next year. The line manager should:

- discuss the scope of the job, for example the job description, the employee's responsibilities, and any changes to them.
- find out the employee's opinion of their performance, and then present their own assessment supported by evidence.
- set SMART – **S**pecific, **M**easurable, **A**ttainable, **R**elevant, and **T**imed – objectives for the coming year.

Conversation

92

Caterina Black, a senior manager at Chesham Pharmaceuticals, is giving one of her team leaders, Edward Ward, his annual performance review.

Caterina: So, first of all, I'd like to check if we're on the same page regarding your responsibilities. You supervise the sales staff for the whole south-eastern region, you're a member of the European sales committee, and you coordinate the cooperation between the production team and marketing. **Have I missed anything?**

Edward: Don't forget, I'm captain of the company's basketball team as well!

C: Of course not! Especially after you won the Intercompany Cup in April. **Would you like to add anything else?**

E: No, I think that's covered pretty much everything.

C: Good. So, **how do you feel about your performance this year?**

E: Well, quite good. I hit all my sales targets we set in last year's review.

C: Yes, that's true. **My impression is that** you enjoy that part of your work most.

E: Hmm, well that is my main responsibility.

C: Quite right. However, working together with the production department is very important and **I've observed that** the cooperation between marketing and production hasn't really improved. We still seem to have the same problems that we had last year.

E: I'm not quite sure what you mean.

C: Production still complains about lack of advance information from us.

E: Well, they are just so inflexible.

C: I quite agree. But the bottom line is, we have to work together. So, **I would like you to establish** a job rotation scheme. I want two salespeople to spend six months in production and two people from production to replace them in our sales team. That way, both departments will get a better idea of what needs to be done.

E: Oh... but they won't know any of our customers!

C: Well, you'll have to train them. **I expect you to organize this by** the end of the month.

E: The end of the month?!

C: Yes. I've spoken to Tom Wilkinson in production and he agrees with me that this is the best way forward. He'll set up a meeting with you for later this afternoon.

E: I see. Well, perhaps it will help.

C: Good. Now, let's move on to discuss your development. **Looking ahead,** I think it would be a good idea if you took part in some project management training.

E: Sure. It's definitely something I'm interested in.

C: Good, because **down the line,** project work is going to be where the best opportunities for promotion are in our company. And I feel **you need to develop your leadership skills.**

E: Definitely. I mean I would really appreciate any opportunities I get to improve on that aspect of my work.

Understanding

Are these statements true or false?

1 Caterina asks Edward how he feels he has performed this year.
2 She asks him if he has any problems at work.
3 She asks him what he thinks about the production department.
4 She describes the various aspects of his job and makes sure that he agrees.
5 She discusses his professional development for the future.
6 She sets him a specific objective to meet.
7 She tells him about the future plans for the company.
8 She tells him how she feels he has performed this year.
9 She tells him that she is disappointed with his performance.
10 She asks him for feedback on how his team has performed this year.

Saying it accurately

1 **Read these interviewer questions and statements. Group them in the correct categories, following the example.**

Discussing employee's job description: *1*
Assessing employee's performance:
Setting employee an objective:
Discussing employee's future development:

1 Are you happy with how I've outlined your job description?
2 Down the line, I think it would be helpful for you to develop your interpersonal skills.
3 Have I missed out anything that you do in your position?
4 How do you feel about your performance this year?
5 I expect you to have completed your review of expenses by Tuesday.
6 I would like you to organize an employee First Aid course by January.
7 I've observed that you are steadily improving in all areas of your job.
8 Is that a fair description of your role?
9 Looking ahead, I think you should work to improve your leadership skills.

10 Moving forward, perhaps we could look at management training courses.

11 My impression is that your performance has way exceeded our expectations this year.

12 Please could you set up a meeting with all the relevant personnel by the end of the week?

2 **Complete the conversation with sentences from *Saying it accurately 1*. In some places, more than one answer is possible.**

Manager:	And so, as personnel assistant, your responsibilities include writing advertisements for vacancies, selecting possible candidates, and sitting in on the interviews with the relevant manager. *1*
Employee:	Yes, that's right, but I also carry out induction days for new employees and some in-house training for existing employees.
Manager:	Oh yes, of course. ....
Employee:	Well, I think I've done well. I've helped to recruit twenty-three new members of staff and carried out successful inductions with all of them.
Manager:	Yes, I've had some positive feedback on that. As for my personal opinion, ...
Employee:	That's very encouraging to hear.
Manager:	Great. Right, some employees have mentioned to me that they would like to receive First Aid training. I'm all in favour of that so ....
Employee:	OK. Should that be open to everyone in the company?
Manager:	Yes, absolutely. OK, ...
Employee:	Yes, I'd be very keen to go on a management course. Thanks.

Saying it clearly

93 **1** **Listen to these sentences, noting the different pronunciations of 's' and 'th'.**

*I've observed **th**at you hit all your **s**ales targets.*

*Have I mi**ss**ed out any area**s** **th**at you'd like to develop?*

*I**s** **th**ere any**th**ing el**s**e **th**at you'd like to discu**ss**?*

*Moving forward, I **th**ink **th**at we should look at management course**s**.*

2 **Listen again to the sentences from *Saying it clearly 1* and repeat them.**

Saying it appropriately

94 **1** **Listen to the speakers. How do they sound?**

1 interested or uninterested

2 negative or positive
3 polite or impolite; assertive or shy
4 diplomatic or blunt; angry or encouraging

94 **2** **Listen to the sentences from *Saying it appropriately 1* and repeat them.**

Get speaking

95 **1** **You are carrying out a performance review with your office manager, Kamil. Play the audio CD and follow the cues. You start.**

1 Outline Kamil's job description (in the following bullet points) and ask if he agrees to:
   - maintaining office services
   - supervising office staff
   - overseeing office records and efficiency.

   Ask if you have missed anything.
2 Ask him about his opinion of his performance this year.
3 Agree with what Kamil says and give him positive feedback on his performance this year.
4 Set him an objective regarding the implementation of the second phase of the office refurbishment: new furniture and equipment for the ground floor. Make sure that it meets the SMART requirements.
5 Move the conversation on to talk about the future and suggest that Kamil should develop his IT skills and suggest training on this.

2 **Think about your own workplace. Write a list of employees for whom you carry out performance reviews.**

1 Outline the jobs of the employees that you have listed. How might you describe these in a performance review? Practise them aloud.
2 How have the employees performed this year? Say a sentence about each of them as you might in their performance review.
3 Think of an objective (real or imaginary) for each of the employees and make sure that it meets the SMART requirements. Practise them aloud.

Language note

*Well, **quite** good,* meaning 'to a degree/fairly/rather'.

***Quite** right,* meaning 'completely'.

*I'm not **quite** sure,* meaning 'completely'.

*I **quite** agree,* meaning 'completely'.

In British English, 'quite' usually means 'to a degree/fairly/rather', for example, '*the conference was **quite** short.*'

In American English, 'quite' usually means 'completely' or 'very', for example, '*the conference was **quite** fascinating.*'

20 Persuading your manager

Would you be willing to support my request?

USEFUL TIPS: If you want to ask for something special from your manager, you need to be well prepared.

- Be proactive. Ask your manager for a meeting to discuss what is on your mind.
- Persuade, don't threaten. Decide what exactly you want and be prepared to justify your demands with logical arguments, rather than emotional ones.
- Be ready to negotiate. Think in advance about the best alternative to your preferred solution.
- Remain polite. Whatever the result, always thank your manager for their time at the end of the meeting. You still have to work with them.

Conversation

96

Candy is a highly skilled programmer in a large software company. She wants to discuss an issue with her manager, John.

Candy: Hi John! Do you have a moment?

John: Sure, Candy. What can I do for you?

C: **I'd like to schedule a meeting with you to talk about my position.** When's a good time for you?

J: Er, well, it's probably best if you fix a time with my secretary, OK?

C: Fine. I'll do that.

J: Come in, Candy, take a seat. Now, what can I do for you?

C: Well, **I'd like to discuss my compensation package with you.**

J: Really? I thought you were happy with the increase we gave you last year!

C: Yes, but **I hope you'll agree that** since last year I've achieved such a lot and we need to consider these achievements. For example, I was responsible for organizing the conference in Astana last month and...

...and finally, I managed the ISO 9001 audit, which we successfully completed. So, **wouldn't you agree that my performance this year has been** very successful?

J: Well, yes. But what exactly do you want?

C: I understand that this year the pay increase is between 3 and 8 per cent. **I would like to ask** for a raise at the top end of that scale.

J: Ooh! I don't know about that, Candy, I mean, what about the others?

C: If you look at my responsibilities in comparison to my colleagues, I am currently underpaid. **Wouldn't you say this should be taken into consideration?**

J: I'm not sure that that is really quite true, Candy.

C: Oh, I think so. I checked. Compared to programmers in other companies, I'm earning about 4 per cent less than the market average. Here are the figures.

J: Are you saying you want to leave?

C: No, I just want you to know the background to my request, that's all. **I'm sure you can see that** it wouldn't be hard for me to get a better paid job elsewhere.

J: I see.

C: So, **would you be willing to support my request for** a higher wage increase?

J: Well, the problem is also your qualifications. Even though you are a fantastic programmer, you don't have the qualifications on paper for me to justify to the HR department putting you into a higher salary level.

C: **I thought that might be a problem.** So, **wouldn't it make sense for** the company to invest in sending me on an advanced programming skills course? The company benefits from my improved skills, I have the necessary qualifications on paper and you could then justify to the HR department paying me more. I hope you'll agree that that would be a win-win situation for everybody.

J: Hmm. I need to think about this idea.

C: Sure. I'll find a time for another meeting towards the end of the week with your secretary. But **thanks for your time today.** I do appreciate that.

Understanding

Tick the statements that are true about Candy and John.

1 She agrees with her boss that she doesn't have the qualifications on paper and accepts that this will mean she can't get a top-end pay rise.
2 She becomes emotional, telling him how much she loves her job.
3 She negotiates with regard to her lack of qualifications on paper.
4 She demands additional training.
5 She is polite and thanks her boss for his time.
6 She reminds him that he promised her a good pay rise last year.
7 She presents logical arguments on why should she receive a top-end pay rise.
8 She says that she will look for another job if he won't give her a pay rise.
9 She schedules a meeting with her boss.
10 She stops by to see her boss unannounced.

Saying it accurately

Match the two halves of the sentences.

1 I think you'll agree that…
2 I'd like to ask for…
3 Would you be willing to…
4 I'd like to schedule a meeting with you…
5 Wouldn't you say this should be…
6 I'd like to discuss my…
7 Wouldn't it make sense for…
8 Thanks for…
9 I thought that might be a problem…
10 I wanted to ask you if it…

A …a transfer to a different department.
B … your time today. I do appreciate that.
C …me to attend a management training course?
D …compensation package with you.
E …my proposal for unpaid leave is quite convincing.
F …support my request for extended leave?
G …would be possible for me to extend my paternity leave?
H …taken into consideration?
I …to discuss my position.
J …, so perhaps you would consider this proposal?

Saying it clearly

97 **1** **Listen to the statements from *Saying it accurately.* Repeat them, copying the rhythm of the speaker.**

98 **2** **Listen and compare these similar sounds from the unit.**

1. 'ch'	2. 'j'	3. 's'	4. 'z'
achieved such much	managed job suggestions	discuss sense skills	organizing raise skills

3 **Listen again to the words from *Saying it clearly 2* and repeat them.**

Saying it appropriately

99 **1** **When you are trying to persuade your manager to agree to something, use an appropriate tone of voice: polite, confident, and persuasive. Which of the following speakers use an appropriate tone?**

speaker 1
speaker 2
speaker 3
speaker 4
speaker 5
speaker 6
speaker 7
speaker 8
speaker 9
speaker 10

100

2 **Listen again to the speakers from *Saying it appropriately 1*. This time, they will all use an appropriate tone. Repeat what they say.**

Get speaking

101

1 **You would like a transfer to the US office. Play the audio CD and follow the cues. You start.**

1 Ask your boss, Karen, if you can schedule a meeting with her.
2 Thank her and explain your request.
3 Remind her that you've been a loyal employee over the last six years and explain how you are keen for a new challenge and the opportunity to live abroad.
4 Say that you've considered this point and were wondering if anyone from the US office would consider a job swap for a few months.
5 Thank her for her time.

2 **Write a short dialogue similar to the one in *Get Speaking 1*. Imagine a situation in your workplace and replace the request for a transfer with one you might make. Practise the dialogue aloud.**

Cultural note

In some cultures, there is more respect for hierarchy than in others. This means that employees in some countries are less likely to approach their managers with a difficult issue than employees in other countries. This is worth bearing in mind when working across cultures.

Grammar note

Note how Candy uses questions to make her language sound more persuasive. She forms most of these with the modal verb *wouldn't*, which implies that John will agree with the point that she is making. This makes her sound confident and persuasive.

Examples from the text:

Wouldn't you say this should be taken into consideration?

Wouldn't it make sense for the company to invest in sending me on an advanced programming skills course?

Wouldn't you agree that my performance this year has been very successful?

APPENDIX – Extended learning through COBUILD

This section provides you with information from the COBUILD corpus on key vocabulary items in the conversations. It gives information on meaning, usage and collocations.

Unit 1 Starting a conversation

exactly

- When I left school, I wasn't sure exactly what I wanted to do.
- It is difficult to explain exactly what it is.
- I do exactly what stockbrokers do.

COLLOCATIONS: **do/know/understand/define/explain** *something* exactly
exactly **right/sure/correct**
exactly **match/mirror/replicate** *something*

SYNONYM: precisely

Unit 2 Talking about jobs

challenging

- We continue to face a challenging retail environment.
- After ten years, I still find my job immensely challenging and satisfying.
- My last job wasn't mentally challenging.

COLLOCATIONS: a challenging **role/task/environment/marketplace**
extremely/incredibly/immensely challenging
intellectually/mentally/physically challenging

SYNONYMS: demanding, rigorous

rewarding

- Teaching is a worthwhile and rewarding career.
- It's hugely rewarding when you can sort out a problem for someone.
- Real estate is an industry I've found financially and emotionally rewarding.

COLLOCATIONS: a rewarding **job/career/profession/pursuit/endeavour/experience**
richly/hugely/immensely/highly rewarding
financially/emotionally/spiritually rewarding

SYNONYMS: gratifying, satisfying, stimulating

Unit 3 Showing interest in other people

negotiation

- It's a matter for negotiation between an employer and their workforce.
- We're currently in negotiations over a new contract.

COLLOCATIONS: negotiation(s) **between** *people*
negotiation(s) between **management/staff/employers/workers/representatives**
negotiations **over** *something*
negotiations over a **contract/issue/settlement**
negotiations over **pay/payment/compensation**
negotiations **with** *someone*
negotiations with a **supplier/vendor/buyer/developer/creditor**

SYNONYMS: discussion, dialogue

PHRASES: under negotiation, subject to negotiation, open to negotiation, in negotiations

Unit 4 Exchanging information

apparently

You use **apparently** to indicate that the information you are giving is something that you have heard, but you are not certain that it is true.

- Apparently, all new manufacturing is to take place in eastern Europe.
- Apparently, the meeting today was very positive.
- He resigned, apparently because of disagreements with his boss.

SYNONYMS: seemingly, supposedly

Unit 5 Cold calling

risk

- Most investors avoid risk when they can do so without sacrificing return.
- There is a significant risk that the company will fail.
- Most firms are taking risk management seriously.

COLLOCATIONS: **avoid/eliminate/minimize** risks
a **high/potential/significant/serious** risk
a **low/minimal/slight/tiny** risk
a risk **of** *something*
a risk of **failure/injury/death**
a **security/safety/investment/inflation** risk
risk **assessment/management**

Unit 6 Confirming or rearranging appointments

appointment

- Just give me a call and we can arrange an appointment.
- Your appointment is scheduled for tomorrow morning.
- Can I possibly make an appointment for another day?

COLLOCATIONS: **make/request/arrange/book/schedule** an appointment
confirm/cancel/miss/reschedule an appointment
a **scheduled/urgent/available** appointment
an appointments **diary/calendar/book/schedule**
an appointment **with** *someone*
an appointment with a **manager/consultant/specialist/adviser**

Unit 7 Making a complaint on the telephone

unsatisfactory

- I found the service totally unsatisfactory.
- Their behaviour has been wholly unsatisfactory and foolish, to say the least.
- The new charging arrangements are patently unfair and unsatisfactory.

COLLOCATIONS: an unsatisfactory **situation/performance/explanation/outcome**
profoundly/deeply/wholly/thoroughly/totally unsatisfactory
find/consider/deem *something* unsatisfactory

SYNONYMS: inadequate, unacceptable

ANTONYMS: satisfactory, acceptable

Unit 8 Dealing with a complaint on the telephone

refund

- Unfortunately, we can only offer a refund, exchange, or repair if a product is faulty.
- I'm afraid that we cannot offer refunds for cancellations.
- We will replace it or issue a refund, whichever you choose.

COLLOCATIONS: a **full/complete/partial/possible** refund
demand/expect/request/obtain a refund
offer/promise/issue/arrange/give a refund
a refund **policy/offer/guarantee/request**

SYNONYM: reimbursement

Unit 9 Running a face-to-face meeting

agenda

- There are four main points on the agenda of today's meeting.
- Point one on the agenda is to welcome the new staff.
- We may need to postpone some items on the agenda for the next meeting.

COLLOCATIONS: the agenda **for** *something*
the agenda for the **meeting/conference/session**
on the agenda
a **point/item** on the agenda
something **tops/dominates** the agenda
someone **sets/outlines** the agenda

SYNONYMS: plan, programme

Unit 10 Negotiating agreement

proposal

- We would certainly consider any proposals you have in mind.
- I think that's an interesting proposal, but it won't suit everyone.
- We have already discussed several proposals affecting tender offers.

COLLOCATIONS: **submit/present/outline/put forward** a proposal
accept/reject/discuss/consider/review a proposal
a **workable/acceptable/interesting/attractive** proposal
an **unworkable/unacceptable/unrealistic** proposal

SYNONYMS: plan, suggestion, idea

Unit 11 Assigning action points

prioritize

1. If you **prioritize** something, you treat it as more important than other things.

- The company wants to prioritize debt repayments.
- The government is prioritizing the service sector.

2. If you **prioritize** the tasks that you have to do, you decide which are the most important and do them first.

- We'll need to prioritize assignments so that everything continues to run smoothly.
- I tend to prioritize ruthlessly and sacrifice the non-essentials.

Unit 12 Running a teleconference

outsource

- Outsourcing graphic design tasks and printing jobs would make sense for us.
- Cost saving is the big driver for outsourcing work.
- Offshore outsourcing isn't always the cheapest option.

COLLOCATIONS: outsource a **service/function/task/activity**
outsource **work/management/manufacturing/repair**
outsource **offshore/overseas/abroad**

SYNONYM: relocate

Unit 13 Presenting a product or service

advantage

- Our key advantage over competitors is that we manufacture all our products to order.
- This means we are able to take advantage of the very latest costs.
- To take advantage of this incredible offer, you need only visit our website.

COLLOCATIONS: a **distinct/obvious/definite/competitive** advantage
an advantage **of** *something*
take advantage of *something*
take advantage of a **discount/opportunity/offer**
an advantage **over** *someone/something*
an advantage over **competitors/rivals/others**

Unit 14 Working on a stand

customer

- What are you doing to improve your customer services and support?
- You should ask questions in order to understand exactly what the customer wants.
- Customer satisfaction has to be the top priority in all we do.

COLLOCATIONS: a customer **base**
customer **satisfaction/relations/service/feedback**
potential/prospective/existing/loyal customers
attract/target/serve/satisfy/retain customers
customers **of** *something*
customers of **a retailer/store/provider/company**
customers **want/prefer/demand** *something*

SYNONYM: client

Unit 15 Closing a sale

promotion

- We're targeting this promotion at business travellers.
- Our latest promotion offers discounts for passengers who book well ahead of time.
- We're doing a special promotion on champagne.

COLLOCATIONS: **launch/run/hold/target/aim** a promotion
target/aim a promotion **at** *someone*
a promotion **features/includes/involves/offers** *something*
a promotion **helps/encourages/generates/boosts** *something*
a **special/in-store/cut-price/seasonal/sales** promotion

SYNONYM: offer

Unit 16 Saying 'no' politely

order

- You may cancel within 14 days of placing an order.
- We have received 10,000 orders for this digital music player already.
- I can send you our free mail order catalogue.

COLLOCATIONS: **place/make/receive/cancel** an order
a **postal/mail/online/export/minimum** order
an order **for** *something*
an order for **goods/equipment/machinery/items**

Unit 17 The successful job interviewer

position

- Do you see yourself in a management position?
- Wherever possible, senior positions are filled from within the company.
- She has been offered and has accepted the position of managing director.

COLLOCATIONS: **hold/fill/take/accept/advertise/vacate** a position
a **vacant/unfilled/current/full-time/senior/management** position
a position **as** *something*
a position as a **consultant/assistant/clerk/manager/trustee**
a position **within** *something*
a position within a **company/organization/hierarchy**

Unit 18 The successful interview candidate

team

- I head the project management team, overseeing major projects for our clients.
- As a manager, I try to instil a sense of team spirit and togetherness.
- I'm a big team player and I always place an emphasis on the team.

COLLOCATIONS: **lead/head/manage/join** a team
a **capable/confident/talented** team
a **management/design/research** team
a team **player/manager/leader/effort**
team **spirit**

Unit 19 Carrying out performance reviews

opportunity

- There are certainly opportunities for promotion in the company.
- We like to feel that we can offer a lot of career opportunities to our staff.
- I would welcome the opportunity to travel and discuss projects with clients.

COLLOCATIONS: **provide/offer/present/create** an opportunity
seize/welcome/exploit/relish/grasp an opportunity
a **unique/ideal/perfect/good/great** opportunity
a **business/career/networking/marketing** opportunity
an opportunity **for** *something*
an opportunity for **advancement/promotion/growth/input**

Unit 20 Persuading your manager

package

- They've offered a good redundancy package and are confident they'll get enough volunteers.
- The compensation package will be added to staff salaries at the end of January.
- Can you negotiate a package that suits both you and your boss?

COLLOCATIONS: a **compensation/redundancy/severance/retirement** package
offer/unveil/propose/announce a package
negotiate/accept/take/reject a package
a **generous/attractive/acceptable/fair** package
a package **includes/incorporates/combines** *something*

ANSWER KEY

Unit 1

Understanding

Conversation 1 D
Conversation 2 A
Conversation 3 C
Conversation 4 B

Saying it accurately

1

1 been
2 lovely
3 get
4 long
5 means
6 looking
7 from
8 isn't
9 do
10 come

2

[3] Alex: No, it's my first trip.
[6] Sophia: I'm a forensic auditor, which means that I help hedge funds and banks make sure none of their staff are doing anything illegal.
[1] Alex: It's a beautiful day today, isn't it?
[7] Alex: Really? And do you often find any illegal activities?
[2] Sophia: Absolutely, I love New York in the spring. Have you been here before?
[8] Sophia: More than you might expect! Anyway, we'd better get back to the presentation…
[5] Alex: I'm from Athens. It's a great place to live. What do you do?
[4] Sophia: Oh, you must visit the Guggenheim Museum and the Empire State Building. Where do you come from?

4

1 isn't it?
2 Where do you come from?
3 How did you get here?
4 How long did that take?
5 What do you do exactly?

Saying it appropriately

1

1 friendly
2 unfriendly
3 friendly
4 friendly
5 unfriendly

Get speaking

1

(Answers will vary. Suggested answers only.)

I'm a …[insert job title]…, which means that… [add interesting fact about job]… .
I took the plane from Charles de Gaulle.
Only an hour or so. It's a very easy flight.
Yes, it is. Have you been here before?
I'm from …[insert place]… . Did you know that … [add interesting fact about place]…?

2

Answers will vary.

Model answers from *Saying it accurately 2* and *3*.

Unit 2

Understanding

Be brief and precise: '<u>Well, actually I'm a lawyer. I'm in charge of managing the legal department and we make sure that Foodaid understands any legal issues there might be in the work it does.</u>'

Show how your job benefits people: '<u>You feel you are doing something useful with your skills, not just making some company shareholders richer</u>.'

Make it relevant to the person you're talking to: '<u>J: There are lots of different jobs at Foodaid. What subject do you study at university? / S: Engineering. / J: Very important for Foodaid.</u>'

Accentuate the positive: '<u>You'll never be rich working for Foodaid, but you get paid. Very often people like you work with us for a few years to gain experience and then they move onto other jobs. Lots of companies like that.</u>'; '<u>And even if the work is demanding, it's never boring.</u>'

Jenny's mistake was using the acronym 'NGO', which she needed to explain to the student.

Saying it accurately

1

1F 5C
2D 6A
3H 7E
4G 8B

2

(Answers will vary. Suggested answers only.)

2 My job involves helping people to sort out their legal affairs.
3 My main responsibility is to prepare and submit accounts to the tax authorities.
4 I help children who are sick.
5 I'm in charge of looking after the employees at my company.
6 My job entails carrying out research and teaching students at my university.
7 I'm responsible for helping people who are having difficulties with their computers.
8 I develop new and exciting business ideas.

3

1 as
2 in/with
3 with
4 for/in
5 at/for
6 on
7 to
8 for/under

4

(Answers will vary. Suggested answers only.)

1 monotonous
2 rewarding/fulfilling
3 stressful
4 absorbing/interesting/demanding
5 challenging/interesting/fulfilling/absorbing … interesting/stressful/demanding

Saying it clearly

1

(Stressed syllables are underlined.)

1 challenging
2 monotonous
3 rewarding
4 fulfilling
5 interesting
6 stressful
7 absorbing
8 demanding

Saying it appropriately

1

The speakers are very enthusiastic/unenthusiastic, which helps them to accentuate the positive/negative aspects of their jobs.

Get speaking

1 and **2**

Answers will vary. Model answer in *Saying it accurately 1*.

Unit 3

Saying it accurately

1

1 know
2 Really
3 terrible
4 That's
5 How
6 other
7 saying
8 mean

2

To show positive empathy: 1, 3, 6, 7, 9
To show negative empathy: 2, 5, 8, 10
To show disbelief: 4, 9

Note that 9 'How incredible!' has two meanings.

3

1 echoing
2 empathizing
3 paraphrasing
4 empathizing
5 empathizing
6 echoing
7 paraphrasing
8 empathizing

[2] Rachel: How awful!
[1] Rachel: Terrible?
[4] Rachel: That's unbelievable!
[7] Rachel: So what you're saying is I went on holiday for a week and come back to find you're a senior manager?!
[3] Rachel: You mean that you were stuck in traffic for three hours!
[5] Rachel: Really?
[6] Rachel: Promoted?
[8] Rachel: How amazing! Congratulations!

Saying it appropriately

1

In the first extract, Emily's tone is keen/uninterested and her intonation is rising/falling. This response encourages Casper to continue/stop talking about the topic.

In the second extract Emily's tone is keen/uninterested and her intonation is rising/falling. This response encourages Casper to continue/stop talking about the topic.

3

✓ That's wonderful!
✓ Fantastic!
How amazing!
✓ Great!
How terrible!
✓ That's awful!
Oh no!
✓ That's dreadful!
✓ That's unbelievable!
How incredible!

Get speaking

1

(Answers will vary. Suggested answers only.)

1 I see/Really?
2 Next year?
3 So what you're saying is you'd like me to source some possible new offices?
4 Fantastic! / Great!

2

(Answers will vary. Suggested answers only.)

1 That's fantastic! / A new job?
2 Really?
3 How terrible!
4 Late?
5 Fantastic! / You mean you'll be moving to America?
6 Oh no! / Really?

Unit 4

Understanding

Offer appropriate information first: <u>'Christine is so successful. She did an amazing job for us dealing with that whole corruption scandal last year, don't you think?'</u>

Ask questions indirectly: <u>'You used to work for our new chief legal officer, Christine Bender, didn't you?'</u>

Create intimacy: 'I really want to thank you, <u>Michael</u>, for taking me with you to the meeting.'
'You used to work for <u>our</u> new chief legal officer, Christine Bender, didn't you?'
'She did an amazing job for <u>us</u> dealing with that whole corruption scandal last year, don't you think?'

Saying it accurately

1

1 Candy 2 Michael

2

✓ According to Jane…
I'm sure that…
✓ I overheard Ben saying…
✓ Apparently, …
I'm convinced that…
✓ I heard on the grapevine that…
It's certain that…
✓ It seems/appears that…
By all accounts, …
✓ … so I'm told.
It's guaranteed that…
Did you hear that…?
✓ I heard that…

3

(Answers will vary. Suggested answers only.)

2, 3 …so I'm told/by all accounts.
1, 4, 5, 8 Apparently/I heard that/It seems that/ It appears that…
6 According to…
7 Did you hear that…

4

1 You've spent time in our Washington office, haven't you, Jay?
2 You approved our new brochure before it was sent to the printers, didn't you, Rachel?
3 You know our new CEO, don't you, Matt?
4 You're attending our conference this year, aren't you, Lianne?
5 You've seen our budget for next year, haven't you, Dan?

Saying it appropriately

1

question 1: intimate
question 2: direct
question 3: intimate
question 4: intimate
question 5: direct
question 6: intimate

Get speaking

1

(Answers will vary. Model answers only.)

1 I heard on the grapevine / I overheard that the company is planning to set up a sports and social committee, Max.
2 You don't know anything about that, do you Max?
3 Well, according to Janice, the CEO is very enthusiastic about it.

4 You don't know when the meeting might happen, do you Max?
5 You would want to be involved with it, wouldn't you Max?

2

Answers will vary. Dialogue is a model answer.

Unit 5

Understanding

[4] She explains what her company specializes in and the reason for her call.
[1] Macey Chance checks that she is speaking to the correct person.
[6] She sets up a meeting to discuss the matter further.
[2] She introduces herself and says where she works.
[5] She asks questions to gauge the person's interest.
[3] She checks that the person she is speaking to has time to talk.

Saying it accurately

1

A Do you think that's something that might be of interest to you?
B Could we set up a meeting for next week, Mr Lee?
C My company specializes in designing bespoke software.
D This is Tom Sweeney from Lermans and Co.
E May I ask you a question, Mr Lee?
F Do you have a moment to speak to me?

2

1 D
2 F
3 C
4 A
5 E
6 B

3

1 C
2 D
3 E
4 B
5 A

Saying it appropriately

1

1 pushy
2 enthusiastic
3 abrupt
4 friendly
5 polite
6 bored

Get speaking

1

(Answers will vary. Suggested answers only.)

1 Am I speaking to Mr Gulbert?
2 Hello, this is ....[first name] .... [last name] from Top Tier Training.
3 Do you have a moment to speak to me?
4 My company specializes in providing motivational training courses for staff. Do you think that's something that might be of interest to you?
5 Could we set up a meeting for next Tuesday at 10 a.m.?

2

Answers will vary. Model answer in *Get speaking 1.*

Unit 6

Understanding

Tuesday	Wednesday
9 a.m. 10 a.m. 11 a.m. 12 p.m.	9 a.m. 10 a.m. ~~*Gerhard Schmidt, Hippax, Berlin*~~ 11 a.m. 12 p.m.
2 p.m. 3 p.m. *Sabine Gerland, Quiddestrasse* ~~*14*~~ *40* 4 p.m. 5 p.m.	2 p.m. *Teleconference for Gerhard Schimdt and colleague* 3 p.m. 4 p.m. 5 p.m.

Saying it accurately

1

1 confirm
2 check
3 spell
4 better
5 teleconference
6 forward

2

1 C
2 A
3 E
4 B
5 D

Saying it appropriately

1 A
2 B
3 C
4 A

Get speaking

1

(Answers will vary. Suggested answers only.)

The call to Giovanni

1 Hello Mr Fabro, this is ...[first name][last name]... from Marlow Construction. How are you?
2 Fine, thanks. I'm just ringing to confirm our appointment for Wednesday morning at 10 a.m. to discuss the Westdene Hospital building contract.
3 Can I just check the address? That's 40 Findon Street, isn't it?
4 Oh OK, could you spell that for me?
5 Thanks, I look forward to seeing you then. Goodbye.

The call to Joy

6 Hello Ms Lee, this is ...[first name][last name]... from Marlow Construction. How are you?
7 Fine, thanks. I'm just ringing to confirm our appointment for Thursday afternoon at 3 p.m. to update you on the Queen's Hotel building project.
8 No problem. Would Friday at 3 p.m. be more convenient?
9 Great, I look forward to seeing you then. Goodbye.

2

(Answers will vary. Suggested answers only.)

1 Hello, ...[first name][last name]...
2 I'm fine thanks, Valerie. And you?
3 No problem. Would Tuesday be more convenient?
4 Would you like me to arrange a telephone conference instead?
5 Yes, I'll email them over as soon as possible.
6 Goodbye.

Unit 7

Understanding

Strategy	Sentences from the telephone conversation
Make sure you're speaking to the person who can help you.	• Could I speak to your supervisor, please? • Could you tell me your name and position, please? I'll just make a note of that.
State your complaint.	• I need to make a complaint. • I'm afraid I'm not satisfied with...
Set out your expectations to solve the problem.	• I'd like you to...
Confirm when your expectations will be met.	• Could you let me know when you have...? • When will you get back to me?

Saying it accurately

1

1 I'm sorry to say that I'm not satisfied with this product.
2 There appears to be a problem with this product.
3 I'm not at all happy with this service.
4 There seem to be some concerns regarding this product.
5 Please could you replace it?
6 Would you ensure that the replacement is sent today?
7 Would you be able to email me when it has been sent?
8 When can I expect to hear from you?

2

damaged
defective
delayed
disappointing
tolerable
poor
passable
inadequate
mediocre
so-so
indifferent
unacceptable
unprofessional
unreasonable
unsatisfactory
unsuitable

3

<u>forceful</u>
extremely
considerably
very
utterly
entirely
absolutely
totally
completely
altogether

<u>not so forceful</u>
slightly
somewhat
rather
quite

4

(Answers will vary. Suggested answers only.)

1 I need to make a comment about the latest sales figures because they are somewhat/quite/rather/slightly; disappointing/unsatisfactory/mediocre. I'd like you to concentrate your efforts on improving them over the next quarter.
2 There seem to be some concerns regarding the latest delivery, which was extremely/very/considerably delayed. Please could you ensure that it's prompt next time.
3 I'm afraid I'm not at all happy about the budget for the new project, which is altogether/absolutely/

completely/entirely; unsatisfactory/disappointing/ mediocre/indequate. Please could you revise it immediately?
4 There appears to be a problem with the accounts system, which is quite/rather/somewhat/slightly; disappointing/unsatisfactory/mediocre. I'd like you to see that it's fixed by first thing tomorrow.
5 I'm afraid that I'm not satisfied with the new catering company because their food was entirely/ completely/totally/altogether; unsuitable/inadequate/ disappointing. I'd like you to source some alternative suppliers by the start of next week.

Saying it appropriately

1

speaker 1: appropriately
speaker 2: inappropriately
speaker 3: appropriately
speaker 4: inappropriately
speaker 5: inappropriately

Get speaking

1 My name's ...[first name][last name]... and I'm CEO for Rickmans and Co. I want to speak to somebody senior, please.
2 I need to make a complaint.
3 Hello, could I have your name and position, please?
4 I'll just note that down. I hope you can help me.
5 I'm afraid I'm not satisfied with the IT systems that have recently been installed in our offices. Employees haven't received sufficient training and so are finding it very hard to get to grips with the new systems. And the support line, which was supposed to have been available 24 hours a day, has proved unreliable.
6 I would like you to provide additional training for employees and ensure that the support line is staffed 24 hours a day, as agreed.
7 Could you inform me when you've addressed the problem/spoken to him?
8 When can I expect to hear from you?
9 Thank you for your help on this.

Unit 8

Understanding

Tony Hopps – Queen of the Waves

- cabin problems: booked a cabin on the outside, allotted a cabin inside, wife got seasick.
- buffet lunch: finished by the time they arrived at 2 p.m.
- programme changes: fancy-dress party in programme for Saturday night didn't take place.
- laundry: fancy-dress costume got lost in laundry.

Proposed action:

- refund: refund cost of more expensive outside cabin that they didn't receive.
- insurance claim: form on website to complete.
- discount: 10 per cent discount on next booking.

Saying it accurately

1

1G Could you bear with me for 10 minutes while I get to the bottom of what went wrong here?
2C I'm terribly sorry for the problems that you're experiencing.
3H I can imagine that was terrible.
4E I propose that we offer you some sort of compensation.
5A I'll make sure that it gets done by the end of the week.
6D That must have been dreadful.
7F Could you tell me exactly what happened?
8B I do apologize for our part in this.

2 and **3**

Phrases to show regret/empathy: 3H, 6D
Oh dear, I'm sorry to hear that.
You must have felt terrible!

Phrases to find out what the problem is: 1G, 7F
Can you give me the details?
So let me just recap.

Phrases to apologize: 2C, 8B
We would like to apologize to you for these problems.
We are really very sorry for these difficulties.

Phrases to propose a solution/promise action: 4E, 5A
This is what I propose.
We'll deal with that within a week.
We would like to offer you a 10 per cent discount the next time you book an Argonaut holiday as compensation for problems you had. Is that acceptable to you, Mr Hopps?

Saying it appropriately

1

1 Version 1
2 A, D, and E

Get speaking

1

(Answers will vary. Suggested answers only.)

1 I can imagine that was terrible./That must have been dreadful. Oh dear, I'm sorry to hear that.
2 Could you bear with me for 10 minutes while I get to

the bottom of what went wrong here?
3 I'm terribly sorry for the problem that you experienced./I do apologize for our part in this./ We are really very sorry for these difficulties.
4 I propose that we offer you some sort of compensation./We would like to offer you .... as compensation for .... Is that acceptable to you, Mr/Ms ...[last name]...?

2

(Answers will vary. Suggested answers only.)

1 Oh dear, I'm sorry to hear that. Could you tell me exactly what happened?
2 That must have been dreadful!
3 So let me just recap. The food was delivered late, the waiting staff were not very professional and the food itself was not up to our usual standards?
4 I'm terribly sorry for the problems that you've had. I'll ensure that all the issues you've raised are addressed.
5 I propose that we offer you a 5 per cent discount on your next order as compensation. Is that acceptable to you, Mr Grant?
6 OK, shall we say a 10 per cent discount? How does that sound?
7 I won't let it happen again. Thank you for your call. Goodbye.

3

Answers will vary. Dialogue is model answer.

Unit 9

Understanding

So, let's get started. *[ensure good timekeeping]*
Fabian, would you like to start? *[control the discussion]*
So, to sum up point number one, *[summarize key decisions]*
Let's move onto the next point: budget. *[ensure good timekeeping]*
Tony, that's your field. *[control the discussion]*
Can I stop you there, Fabian? Let's not get sidetracked. Let Tony tell us what exactly is planned and then we can... *[control the discussion]*
We all have our action points to deal with and we know the next steps. *[summarize key decisions]*
How does everybody feel about that? *[control the discussion]*
So, that wraps up everything for today. *[ensure good timekeeping]*

The one tip that Janette does not follow: she does not go through the agenda at the start of the meeting.

Saying it accurately

1

1 coming, down
2 make, start
3 welcome, started
4 aim, fix
5 agenda, points
6 see
7 look, point
8 begin/start
9 kick/start
10 sidetracked
11 sight
12 on
13 thoughts
14 agree
15 think
16 up
17 agreed
18 sum

Get speaking

1

1 I'm glad you could both make it. Perhaps we could make a start.
2 The aim of this meeting is to discuss plans for the upcoming company conference. On the agenda today are the following points for discussion: one, the program for the day and two, possible locations.
3 So, let's look at point number one on the agenda, the program for the day. Rita, would you like to start?
4 I like that idea, Rita. What do you think, Paolo?
5 Yes, that's great. Would you be willing to come up with some detailed suggestions for the type of sessions that we could offer?
6 Shall we move onto the next point: possible locations for the conference? Any thoughts on this, Rita?
7 Can I stop you there, Paolo? Let's not get sidetracked. So, tell us more about the conference facilities at the racetrack, Rita.
8 Sounds promising, Rita. Could you get some prices for us?
9 Shall I go over the main points that we've agreed? With regard to the program for the day, we think it would be good for middle managers to give the presentations this year and Paolo is going to come up with some ideas for some interactive sessions for the rest of the employees. And with regard to location, Rita is going to get some prices on the conference venue at the racetrack. Is everyone happy with that?
10 Would anyone like to add anything?
11 OK, that wraps up everything for today.

Unit 10

Understanding

Stage	Sentences from the conversation
1 Proposal	We suggest that we pay you €700 per head per day.
2 Clarification of proposal	We need to talk about fees.
3 Counter-proposal	Well, that's an interesting proposal, but €700 per day is far too low. €950 is nearer the mark.
4 Discussion	Let's think about how we can make this work.
5 Suggestions of alternatives	Another possibility might be to have two rates: €650 for the programmers and €950 for the others. But have you considered the advantages of just one single flat rate?
6 New proposal	If we agree on a daily rate of €750 per head per day over six months, your company will receive €772,000.
7 Agreement	I take your point. We can live with that.

Saying it accurately

1

1 E
2 C
3 B
4 F
5 A
6 D

2

(Suggested answers.)

1 we need to talk about
2 We propose/suggest that
3 that's not going to work for us
4 another possibility might be to
5 We suggest/propose that
6 I don't think we could go along with that/That's not going to work for us
7 we can live with that

Get speaking

1

(Suggested answers.)

1 We need to talk about what exactly that price would include.
2 I don't think we could go along with that. We propose that we pay you $150,000 inclusive of materials.
3 That's an interesting proposal, but I don't think that's going to work for us. We suggest that we pay you $160,000 including materials. Have you considered the advantages of working with us. We're planning to renovate our offices all over the country next year, so this could lead to a great deal more work in the future.

Unit 11

Understanding

Employee	Task(s) allocated	Finish date/ time
Tony	• *Taking care of Dimitri Mischkovic during his stay* • *Writing report on business activities for last twelve months.*	*This weekend* *By Friday midday*
Lucy	• *Running SAP training programme for system users*	*By end September*
Fabian	• *Organizing project kick-off meeting*	*Invitations out by this evening*

Saying it accurately

1

Asking for volunteers to complete a task: 1, 6, 7, 9, 15
Allocating a task to a particular person: 2, 4, 8, 12, 14
Determining a completion time for the task: 3, 5, 10, 11, 13

2

1 of
2 in
3 for
4 about
5 by
6 with

3

1 Is anyone interested in doing this? / Who would like to take responsibility for this?
2 ...can you take care of that? / ...will you deal with that for me?
3 When do you think the statements will be ready by?

Saying it appropriately

1

1 impolitely
2 politely
3 politely
4 impolitely
5 impolitely
6 politely

Get speaking

1

(Suggested answers only.)

1 Is anyone interested in writing the pitch for the new project? Could you handle that, Jessica? Will you be able to get it done by Friday?
2 I need somebody to source samples for the new company logo. Would anyone like to put themselves forward for this? Chris, could you take care of that? Is the end of the month realistic as a deadline?
3 I'm looking for somebody to prepare a quotation for a new client, Millwood and Co. Can I leave that with you, Ayisha? Can you send that out by next Thursday?
4 Are there any volunteers to write an advertisement to go in the paper for a new office manager? Would you take responsibility for that, Dan? Will you be able to get it done by the end of the day?
5 We need to decide who is going to organize the purchase and delivery of the new IT hardware. Who would like to take responsibility for this? Could you deal with that, Sophie? Is November realistic as a deadline?

Unit 12

Understanding

At the start, Janette laid out ground rules. She asked speakers to:

- give their name first so they knew who was speaking
- not interrupt other speakers
- speak clearly
- let her know if anything was unclear.

Carlo interrupted Petra when she was talking about software testing.
Lee Ming asked Sanjay to clarify what he meant by working 'closely' together.
Everyone agreed on an action point to start discussions with key suppliers in Mumbai.
Another teleconference is booked.

Saying it accurately

1

1 So, it's Karen here.
2 Thank you all for participating today.
3 Before we start, let's just lay out some ground rules for telephone conferences.
4 Firstly, please always give your name first.
5 Secondly, don't interrupt other speakers, please.
6 Thirdly, Please could you make sure that you speak clearly.
7 Finally, just let me know if anything is unclear.
8 Right, let's run through the agenda.

2

1 interrupt
2 finish
3 sorry
4 speaker
5 come
6 there
7 finished
8 let

3

1 B
2 D
3 A
4 C

Saying it appropriately

1

1 impolite
2 polite
3 polite
4 impolite

Get speaking

1

(Answers will vary. Suggested answer only.)

So, it's …[first name][last name]… here. Thank you all for participating today. Before we start, let's just lay out some ground rules for telephone conferences. Please always give your name first, so that we all know who's speaking. Also, don't interrupt other speakers, please. I'll make sure that we keep the conversation on track and don't lose any time. Finally, please could you make sure that you speak clearly and let me know if anything is unclear. OK?

2

1 Excuse me Emin, but I don't think Pierre has finished yet.
2 Sorry Jake, could you repeat that using clearer terms, please?
3 Excuse me, Pierre, but I'm afraid I missed that. Could you say it again, please?
4 Excuse me, is that acceptable to you, Emin?
5 Sorry, can I just come in here? One speaker at a time, please.

3

Answers will vary. Model answer in dialogue and *Get speaking 1*.

Unit 13

Understanding

1 B
2 A
3 C

Saying it accurately

1

3, 2, 1

2

1 C
2 A
3 B
4 G
5 E
6 D
7 F

3

My talk today is about/I want to tell you today about Telesmart, a new communications package that we're offering to our loyal customers. First of all,/Firstly, I'll demonstrate how it works. Next,/Then I'll outline the advantages compared to other packages available and, finally,/lastly, I'll show you how it can benefit your business…

…which means that you can combine all your business communications in one single package. Why is this important? Because it is much more straightforward than having a number of different providers for each service. Let's look now at/Moving onto my next point, how much money this can save you every year…
…and so, to sum up,/in conclusion, Telesmart is a convenient way of saving you money. Thank you for your time. Now over to you, please feel free to ask questions./if anybody has any questions, I'd be happy to answer them.

Saying it appropriately

1

Sentences 1, 4, and 6 are true. The rest are false.

Get speaking

1

Answers will vary. Model answers in dialogue and *Saying it accurately 1*.

2

Answers will vary.

Unit 14

Understanding

Colin
Field of business: Specialist stamp collecting book publisher.
Customers: Children, teenagers, adults, people who have retired, mostly male.
Customers looking for: information and books about stamps.
Challenges: Reaching customers all over the world.
Add to mailing list? Yes
To do: send copy of demo software

Saying it accurately

1

(Answers will vary. Suggested answers only.)

1 What line of work are you in?
2 What does that involve exactly?
3 What sort of customers do you have?
4 What do your customers want?
5 What would help you to help your customers?
6 What issues do you face in your line of work?

2

1 B
2 F
3 D
4 E
5 C
6 A

3

(Order of questions/answers may vary, but answers must follow correct questions.)

[12] **Kay:** Well, would you be interested in hearing more about our website design service? It would be a great way to publicize your services.
[2] **Kay:** Hello Jon, nice to meet you. First of all, what line of work are you in?
[4] **Kay:** And what does that involve exactly?
[3] **Jon:** I'm a surveyor.
[6] **Kay:** What sort of customers do you have?
[13] **Jon:** Yes, I would.
[14] **Kay:** Here's some more information on that then. And can I add you to our mailing list?
[5] **Jon:** Well, I carry out valuations and building surveys on properties for clients.
[15] **Jon:** That sounds like a good idea. I think it would be useful to keep up-to-date with any new PR ideas.

[10] **Kay:** What challenges do you face in your line of work?
[8] **Kay:** And what do your customers want from you?
[1] **Jon:** Hello Kay, I'm Jon.
[11] **Jon:** We find it hard to get our message out to new clients without spending lots of money on advertising.
[7] **Jon:** Mainly small businesses or private purchasers.
[9] **Jon:** They are looking for a professional service, which is delivered promptly and is good value for money.

Saying it appropriately

1

speaker 1 C
speaker 2 A
speaker 3 B

2

Speaker 3 is likely to generate most interest because of the style of their approach.

3

1 I'm [really] sorry but I haven't got any brochures left.
2 Unfortunately I forgot to bring my business cards. I do [apologize].
3 I'm [afraid] I can't help on you on this. I'll ask a colleague.

Get speaking

(Answers will vary. Suggested answers only.)

1 Hello, can I help you?
2 What line of work are you in?
3 Who are your customers?
4 What do your customers want?
5 What challenges do you face in your line of work?
6 Would you be interested in hearing about a new video link teleconferencing system that would allow you to have meetings with customers around the world?

Unit 15

Understanding

conversation 1: urgent close
conversation 2: hard close
conversation 3: emotional close
conversation 4: urgent close

Saying it accurately

1

1 How do you think it will look when it's installed?
2 How many can I put you down for?
3 It's only available at this price today.
4 Shall we start the paperwork?
5 We only have this offer for a short time.
6 We've only got six of this item left in stock.
7 What will people say when they see it?
8 What will you feel like when it's in place?
9 When would you like to start?

2

a hard close: 2, 4, 9
an emotional close: 1, 7, 8
an urgent close: 3, 5, 6

Saying it appropriately

3

(Answers will vary. Suggested answers only.)

1 Seller's mistake: Seller should not use closed questions. They should frame the request or sales pitch in an open way.
Seller should have said: It's a great opportunity. Shall we start the paperwork?
2 Seller's mistake: Seller should assume customer wants to buy the product. Seller should not allow customer an easy way out.
Seller should have said: When would you like to start?
3 Seller's mistake: Seller should be quiet and let customer decide.
Seller should have said: How many can I put you down for?

Get speaking

(Suggested answers.)

1 We have a special offer on this. The 24-hour call-out feature is included in the basic package at no additional cost. But we only have this offer for a short time.
2 And so we can do £8.99 per head for the full buffet. Shall we start the paperwork?
3 It's only €10,000 to supply hand-made Swedish desks and chairs throughout the whole office. What will you feel like when you can see the stunning designs in place?
4 Our fee is $10,000 for the whole audit. When would you like us to start?
5 That means it costs only $5,000 a unit when you order more than twenty. I should point out though that there are only fifty units left in stock. Otherwise, you'll have to wait three months till the next shipment.

6 And corporate membership will work out at only £30 a month. How do you think your employees will feel when you tell them those amazing rates?

Unit 16

Understanding

Conversation 1

C1: I'm really sorry, [Uses emphasizers, for example, 'really' with 'sorry'] but that's not possible. Company policy doesn't allow me to make that kind of deal. [Outside circumstances.]

C1: No, I'm sorry, [Apology] I have an appointment in ten minutes. I don't really have the time right now. [Outside circumstances.]

Conversation 2

C2: Unfortunately, that's just not possible. [Apology] I'm a freelance journalist, so I really don't need three licences. [Explanation.]

C2: Sorry, but that's out of the question. [Apology] I'd lose my job! We have to keep our independence from the computer industry. [Outside circumstances/ explanation.]

Saying it accurately

1

1 sorry
2 possible
3 work
4 not
5 rather
6 no
7 time
8 back
9 thanks
10 question

2

1 No, I'm sorry. Note that all sentences from *Saying it accurately 1* would fit here.
2 Unfortunately, that's just not possible … /I'm really sorry, but that's not going to work…
3 I'm afraid I don't really have the time now…
4 Sorry, but that's out of the question.

Saying it appropriately

1

1 B
2 A
3 B
4 A

2

speaker 1: sincere
speaker 2: insincere
speaker 3: insincere
speaker 4: sincere
speaker 5: insincere

Get speaking

1

(Answers will vary. Suggested answers only.)

1 No, I'm afraid not. We just don't have the budget to purchase additional software this year.
2 I'm really sorry, but I can't change company budgeting policy.
3 Sorry, but it's out of the question. Goodbye.

2

Answers will vary. Model answers in *Get speaking 1*.

Unit 17

Understanding

1

To find out about the candidate's:	Questions from dialogue
personality	• What are your weaknesses, would you say?
goals and ambitions	• What are your goals for the next five years?
work history	• What do you feel has been your biggest achievement to date? • Why would you like to leave your current job?
suitability for company and role	• What do you know about our company? • What makes you suitable for this job, do you think? • What is good customer service, in your view?

2

Georgina Harris comments on Mansha Khan's age when saying 'Well, you are quite young, aren't you?'

Saying it accurately

1

1 hire
2 independently
3 yourself
4 situation
5 greatest
6 rewarding
7 challenges
8 current
9 see
10 right

2

1 Why do you think you're right for this job?/What makes you suitable for this job, do you think?/Why should I hire you for this job?
2 What do you know about our company?
3 What are your greatest strengths and weaknesses?
4 What has been most rewarding about your current job?/What do you feel has been your biggest achievement to date?
5 So why would you like to leave your current job?
6 Where do you see yourself in five years' time?/ What are your goals for the next five years?

Saying it appropriately

1

Appropriate questions: 1, 4, 7, 10. The rest are inappropriate questions.

Get speaking

(Answers will vary. Suggested answers only.)

1 Thanks for coming today, it's nice to meet you. What makes you suitable for this job, do you think?
2 OK, great. And what are your greatest strengths and weaknesses?
3 Uh-huh, could you give me an example of a time when you had to multitask in your current role?
4 That's good. And why would you like to leave your current job?
5 Right. And what are your goals for the next five years?
6 That's interesting. Thanks for your time. We'll be in touch.

Answers will vary with regard to employing this candidate, but most people would probably think that the candidate answered the questions effectively.

Unit 18

Understanding

Candidate	Would you hire this candidate?	Why/Why not?
1	Yes	He effectively expands on details in his résumé and talks about his relevant experience in depth.
2	No	He does not reply using full sentences and so offers no useful or convincing information about his suitability for the job, even when pressed.
3	Yes	She demonstrates that she has researched the background of the company and emphasizes the positive aspects.
4	Yes	She answers the question honestly and shows that she is aware of her weakness and working to improve it.
5	No	He misinterprets the question and does not listen when the interviewer tries to correct him.

Saying it accurately

1

1 E
2 F
3 B
4 H
5 G
6 D
7 A
8 C

2

There are no correct answers here. It depends on your opinion of yourself.

Saying it clearly

1

conscientious
creative
dependable
determined
diplomatic
enthusiastic
experienced
fair
logical
loyal
methodical
motivated
practical
reliable
resourceful
trustworthy

Saying it appropriately

question 1: candidate 2
question 2: candidate 1
question 3: candidate 2
question 4: candidate 2

question 5: candidate 1
question 6: candidate 2
question 7: candidate 1
question 8: candidate 2

Get speaking

1 and **2**

Answers will vary. Model answers in *Saying it accurately 2*.

Unit 19

Understanding

Sentences 1, 4, 5, 6, and 8 are true. The rest are false.

Saying it accurately

1

Discussing employee's job description: 1, 3, 8
Assessing employee's performance: 4, 7, 11
Setting employee an objective: 5, 6, 12
Discussing employee's future development: 2, 9, 10

2

Manager: And so, as personnel assistant, your responsibilities include writing advertisements for vacancies, selecting possible candidates, and sitting in on the interviews with the relevant manager. ...1, 3, 8...

Employee: Yes, that's right, but I also carry out induction days for new employees and some in-house training for existing employees.

Manager: Oh yes, of course. ...4...

Employee: Well, I think I've done well. I've helped to recruit twenty-three new members of staff and carried out successful inductions with all of them.

Manager: Yes, I've had some positive feedback on that. As for my personal opinion, ...7, 11...

Employee: That's very encouraging to hear.

Manager: Great. Right, some employees have mentioned to me that they would like to receive First Aid training. I'm all in favour of that so ...6...

Employee: OK. Should that be open to everyone in the company?

Manager: Yes, absolutely. OK, ...10...

Employee: Yes, I'd be very keen to go on a management course. Thanks.

Saying it appropriately

1

1 interested
2 positive
3 polite; assertive
4 diplomatic; encouraging

Get speaking

1

(Answers will vary. Suggested answers only.)

1 So, your main responsibilities are maintaining office services, supervising office staff, and overseeing office records and efficiency. Have I missed anything, Kamil?
2 How do you feel about your performance this year?
3 Yes, absolutely. My impression is that your performance has been very good this year.
4 I'd like you to implement the second phase of the office refurbishment, namely new furniture and equipment for the ground floor, by [indicate a deadline] March of next year.
5 Great. Moving forward, I think you should work to improve your IT skills. Perhaps we could look at training courses for that?

2

Answers will vary. Model answers in dialogue.

Unit 20

Understanding

Sentences 3, 5, 7, and 9 are true. The rest are false.

Saying it accurately

1 E
2 A
3 F
4 I
5 H
6 D
7 C
8 B
9 J
10 G

Saying it appropriately

1

Those using an appropriate tone are speakers 1, 4, 5, 8, and 9. The rest use an inappropriate tone.

Get speaking

1

(Answers will vary. Suggested answers only.)

1 Excuse me, Karen, I'd like to schedule a meeting with you to discuss my position.
2 Thank you. I wanted to ask you if it would be possible for me to get a transfer to the US office?
3 I appreciate that. But I think you'll agree that I've been a loyal employee over the last six years and I'm very keen now for a new challenge and the opportunity to live abroad.
4 I thought that might be a problem, so perhaps you would consider this proposal. Would you be willing to see if any of the employees in the US office would like to do a job swap for a few months?
5 Thanks for your time today. I do appreciate that.

AUDIO SCRIPTS

Unit 1 Starting a conversation

Track 02

Alex: It's a beautiful day today, isn't it?

Sophia: Absolutely, I love New York in the spring. Have you been here before?

A: No, it's my first trip.

S: Oh, you must visit the Guggenheim Museum and the Empire State Building. Where do you come from?

A: I'm from Athens. It's a great place to live. What do you do?

S: I'm a forensic auditor, which means that I help hedge funds and banks make sure none of their staff are doing anything illegal.

A: Really? And do you often find any illegal activities?

S: More than you might expect! Anyway, we'd better get back to the presentation…

Track 06

So, what do you do exactly?

[beep]

How did you get here?

[beep]

How long did that take?

[beep]

Marseilles's *really* beautiful, isn't it?

[beep]

Where do you come from, then?

[beep]

Unit 2 Talking about jobs

Track 09

1 I'm a nurse. I help to look after people when they are sick.

2 I work in marketing. My main responsibility is to promote new products ahead of their launch.

3 I'm a manager on a construction site. I oversee a team of 250 builders and twenty administrative staff.

4 I'm a PA. My job entails organizing my boss's affairs.
5 I'm an IT programmer. My company develops websites for my clients.
6 I'm a project manager. I'm responsible for making sure that our projects come in on schedule and within budget.
7 I'm an architect. I'm in charge of designing new buildings and pitching ideas to new clients.
8 I'm a banker. My job involves managing my customers' money effectively and profitably.

Unit 3 Showing interest in other people

Track 12

Extract 1:

C: For example, in Singapore you discuss prices much earlier in a negotiation than we do in Germany.

E: Really?

Extract 2:

C: Back in Berlin, I play centre forward for the company football team.

E: Really?

Track 13

C: For example, in Singapore you discuss prices much earlier in a negotiation than we do in Germany.

[beep]

C: Back in Berlin, I play for the company football team.

[beep]

Track 16

I've got some news. I've just found out that they won't renew our lease on this building, so we're going to have to find a new office space.

[beep]

The good thing is that we don't have to be out until the start of next year.

[beep]

And so we've got plenty of time to sort everything out. I'd like you to go away and do some research about potential new sites.

[beep]

That's right. And we should put a bit more in the budget for rent next year.

[beep]

Track 17

1 I've got a new job!
[beep]

2 I've been to Milan three times on business this month. I think it's a beautiful city.
[beep]

3 I went for a walk in my lunch hour and it started to rain and I got soaking wet!
[beep]

4 I missed my train and was late for the meeting.
[beep]

5 I'm being transferred to the New York office.
[beep]

6 My secretary has just resigned.
[beep]

Unit 4 Exchanging information

Track 19

Candy: The company is going to make redundancies next year. Our department will be affected.

Michael: Apparently, the company is going to make redundancies next year. It seems that our department will be affected.

Track 21

1 You used to work for our new chief legal officer, Christine Bender, didn't you?
2 Have you spent time in our Washington office?
3 You approved our new brochure before it was sent to the printers, didn't you, Rachel?
4 You know our new CEO, don't you, Matt?
5 Are you attending our conference this year?
6 You've seen our budget for next year, haven't you, Dan?

Track 22

1 You used to work for our new chief legal officer, Christine Bender, didn't you, Michael?
2 You've spent time in our Washington office, haven't you, Jay?
3 You approved our new brochure before it was sent to the printers, didn't you, Rachel?
4 You know our new CEO, don't you, Matt?
5 You're attending our conference this year, aren't you, Lianne?
6 You've seen our budget for next year, haven't you, Dan?

Track 23

[beep]

Uh-huh.

[beep]

Yeah, I've heard the same thing. But it's something that the board isn't keen on, so I'm told.

[beep]

Well, that's good news. Maybe he'll convince the board in their next meeting.

[beep]

No, I'm afraid not. But I don't think they will approve it this year because they have to wait until the new budget is signed off before making any decisions that might require additional funding.

[beep]

Absolutely, I think it's a great idea.

Unit 5 Cold calling

Tracks 26 and 27

1. Do you think that's something that might be of interest to you?
2. Could we set up a meeting for next week, Mr Lee?
3. My company specializes in designing bespoke software.
4. This is Tom Sweeney from Lermans and Co.
5. May I ask you a question, Mr Lee?
6. Do you have a moment to speak to me?

Track 28

[beep]

Speaking.

[beep]

Oh, yes.

[beep]

Yes, I have a few minutes.

[beep]

The idea sounds interesting.

[beep]

Yes, that sounds good. Look forward to meeting you then.

Unit 6 Confirming or rearranging appointments

Track 31

1 Hello, it's Jan Stevenson here. How are you?
[beep]

2 I'm very well, thank you. But I'm afraid I have to cancel our meeting next Tuesday.
[beep]

3 No, Wednesday isn't any good, I'm afraid, because my partner will be in Shanghai and she really needs to attend too.
[beep]

4 Yes, a telephone conference on Wednesday at 9 a.m. would be great.
[beep]

Track 32

Giovanni Fabro.

[beep]

Hello, I'm well, thanks. And you?

[beep]

Yes, that's right. I'm looking forward to it.

[beep]

No, it's not Findon, it's Fenchurch Street.

[beep]

Of course, F-E-N-C-H-U-R-C-H Street.

Hello, Joy Lee.

[beep]

Very well, thanks. How are you?

[beep]

Ah, I was going to call you today. I'm afraid I can't do Thursday.

[beep]

Yes, that'll be fine.

[beep]

Track 33

[beep]

Hello, this is Valerie Auguste from Finch and Co. How are you?

[beep]

I'm fine. I'm afraid I have to cancel our meeting on Monday.

[beep]

No, I'm afraid I'm out of the country on business then.

[beep]

A telephone conference sounds like a great idea. Will you send me the details?

[beep]

Thank you, I look forward to hearing from you. Goodbye.

[beep]

Unit 7 Making a complaint on the telephone

Track 36

1 I need to make a complaint about the latest sales figures, because they are somewhat disappointing. I'd like you to concentrate your efforts on improving them over the next quarter.

2 There seem to be some concerns regarding the latest delivery, which was extremely delayed. Why is this? Whose fault is it? I want you to get to the bottom of it and tell me who I should shout at.

3 I'm afraid I'm not at all happy about the budget for the new project, which is unsatisfactory. Please could you revise it asap.

4 There appears to be a problem with the accounts system, which is extremely disappointing. Now, you were the one who installed it so I'm holding you personally responsible for this. Sort it out.

5 I'm not satisfied with the new catering company because the food was disgusting. I just can't believe that you hired them. What were you thinking? It was so embarrassing in front of our clients.

Track 37

1 I need to make a complaint about the latest sales figures, because they are somewhat disappointing. I'd like you to concentrate your efforts on improving them over the next quarter.

2 There seem to be some concerns regarding the latest delivery, which was extremely delayed. Please could you ensure it's prompt next time.

3 I'm afraid I'm not at all happy about the budget for the new project, which is unsatisfactory. Please could you revise it asap.

4 There appears to be a problem with the accounts system, which is extremely disappointing. I'd like you to see that it's fixed by first thing tomorrow.

5 I'm afraid that I'm not satisfied with the new catering company because their food was entirely unsuitable. I'd like you to source some alternative suppliers by the start of next week.

Track 38

Receptionist: Hello, Lettermans International, how can I help you?

[beep]

Receptionist: Can I ask what it's regarding?

[beep]

Receptionist: Please hold the line and I'll connect you.

Janet: Hello, Customer Relations.

[beep]

Janet: I'm Janet Green and I'm customer relations manager.

[beep]

Janet: I hope so too. What can I do for you today?

[beep]

Janet: I'm very sorry to hear that. What can we do to improve the situation?

[beep]

Janet: That sounds perfectly reasonable. I'll have a word with our training manager today and set up a time for him to return to the offices.

[beep]

Janet: Of course.

[beep]

Janet: By tomorrow morning, at the latest.

[beep]

Janet: Not at all, we'll get this fixed as soon as we can.

Unit 8 Dealing with a complaint on the telephone

Track 42

1 Could you bear with me for 10 minutes while I get to the bottom of what went wrong here?

2 I'm terribly sorry for the problems you're experiencing.

3 I can imagine that was terrible.

4 I propose that we offer you some sort of compensation.

5 I'll make sure that it gets done by the end of the week.

6 That must have been dreadful.

7 Could you tell me exactly what happened?

8 I do apologize for our part in this.

Track 43

1 And I had to wait for over an hour at the airport before the taxi came to pick me up.

[beep]

2 The whole conference was a farce! Delegates were wandering from room to room and nobody knew where they should be or what was happening. What went wrong?

[beep]

3 And it was all your company's fault.

[beep]

4 So what are you going to do about it?

[beep]

Track 44

Hello, my name is John Grant and I'm afraid there have been several complaints about the food that you supplied for our recent conference.

[beep]

Well, firstly the food was delivered late. It was supposed to be served at 12 p.m. and your staff didn't reach the building until 12.15 p.m. and by the time they started serving, it was 12.30. And speaking of staff, several of your waiters didn't seem to know what they were doing and ended up spilling food all over the place.

[beep]

Anyway, when the food was finally served up it was cold and tasteless. We ordered Chicken Provençal and all we got was a lump of lukewarm meat swimming in a bland sauce with a few limp tomatoes. Not very impressive.

[beep]

Yes, that's about the sum of it.

[beep]

OK.

[beep]

Frankly, that doesn't seem enough.

[beep]

OK, I suppose that's acceptable. As long as you can assure us that we won't have the same problems again.

[beep]

Unit 9 Running a face-to-face meeting

Track 46

1 Thank you all for coming. Let's get down to business.
2 I'm glad you could all make it. Perhaps we could make a start.
3 I'd like to welcome you all here today. Let's get started.
4 The aim of this meeting today is to fix next year's budget.
5 On the agenda today are the following points for discussion.
6 Looking at the agenda, you'll see that there are five things to discuss today.
7 So, let's look at point number one.
8 John, would you like to begin?
9 Lynn, would you like to kick things off?
10 Can you stop there, Paul? Let's not get sidetracked.
11 Let's not lose sight of the main objective here.
12 Shall we move on to the next point?
13 Any thoughts on this, Janine?
14 Do we all agree on this?
15 What do you think, Simon?

16 OK, that wraps up everything for today.

17 So, let's just summarize the main things we've agreed.

18 So, to sum up, we've agreed the budget for next year.

Track 49

Rita: Yes, I've had some thoughts on this. Last year, we had a series of speakers from the senior management team, so we thought that perhaps this year it would be good if we asked some middle managers to do the presentations instead?

[beep]

Paolo: Yes, great idea, as long as the middle managers want to do it, of course! It might be nice to include some interactive sessions for the rest of the employees as well.

[beep]

Paolo: Yes, I'd be happy to.

[beep]

Rita: Um, yes, there's a conference room at the racetrack near the office and I thought that we could look into the possibility of having it there. Speaking of racetracks, did you see the Grand Prix last night? Nail-biting stuff…

Paolo: Yes, it was great. I couldn't believe that last lap…

[beep]

Rita: Sorry, yes, I heard that they have a large conference room and then a separate lounge area alongside.

[beep]

Rita: Sure, no problem.

[beep]

Rita and Paolo: Yes.

[beep]

Rita: No.

Paolo: I don't think so.
[beep]

Unit 10 Negotiating agreement

Track 54

So I reckon we can do the whole job for you, all in at $200,000.

[beep]

Well, that figure would cover manpower and insurance, but not materials, of course.

[beep]

I'm afraid we can't go along with that. Let's think about how we can make this work. Another possibility is to pay us by the day for labour and materials?

[beep]

I take your point… OK, I think we can live with that.

Unit 11 Assigning action points

Note that the text for all the audio is on the page of the unit.

Unit 12 Running a teleconference

Track 60

1 Thank you all for participating today.
2 Before we start, let's just check some ground rules for telephone conferences.
3 Firstly, please always give your name first.
4 Right, let's run through the agenda.
5 Sorry Hans, let Zara finish.
6 One speaker at a time, please.
7 Sorry, can I come in here?
8 Fabrice, I don't think Chris has finished yet.
9 Sorry, but I don't quite follow you. Could you repeat what you just said?
10 Sorry, but I didn't quite catch that. Could you run it by me one more time?
11 Sorry, I'm afraid I missed that. Could you say it again, please?
12 Excuse me, but I'm not sure what you meant by that. Would you mind repeating it?

Track 63

Pierre: It's Pierre here. I'm just not sure that's going to work if we don't —

Emin: This is Emin here. How about we look at —

[beep]

Jake: ...Jake here. I just think it's time to take the bull by the horns on this one.

Kazumi: Excuse me, this is Kazumi. What does 'bull by the horns' mean?

[beep]

Pierre: ...This is Pierre. *[becomes very unclear]*

[beep]

Kazumi: ...Kazumi here. It's just I'm not sure what my manager will say if we go down that route. It depends on a lot of things. I'll have to think about it and look over the figures more carefully. It really is a difficult decision, especially in this climate...

[beep]

Pierre, Emin, Kazumi, and Jake: *[all speaking at once]*

[beep]

Unit 13 Presenting a product or service

Track 66

My talk today is about Telesmart, a new communications package we're offering to our loyal customers. Firstly, I'll demonstrate how it works. Then I'll outline the advantages compared to other packages available and, finally, I'll show you how it can benefit your business...

This means that you can combine all your business communications in one single package. Why is this important? Because it's much more straightforward than having a number of different providers for each service. Let's look now at how much money this can save you every year...

And so, to sum up, Telesmart is a convenient way of saving you money. Thank you for your time. Now over to you. Please feel free to ask questions.

Unit 14 Working on a stand

Track 68

Jon: Hello Kay, I'm Jon.

Kay: Hello Jon, nice to meet you. First of all, what line of work are you in?

Jon: I'm a surveyor.

Kay: And what does that involve exactly?

Jon: Well, I carry out valuations and building surveys on properties for clients.

Kay: What sort of customers do you have?

Jon: Mainly small businesses or private purchasers.

Kay: And what do your customers want from you?

Jon: They are looking for a thorough and professional service, which is delivered promptly and is good value for money.

Kay: What challenges do you face in your line of work?

Jon: We find it hard to get our message out to new clients without spending lots of money on advertising.

Kay: Would you be interested in hearing more about our website design service to publicize what you do?

Jon: Yes, I would.

Kay: Here's some more information on that then. And can I add you to our mailing list?

Jon: That sounds like a good idea. I think it would be useful to keep up to date with any new PR ideas.

Track 69

1 What line of work are you in?
2 What does that involve exactly?
3 What sort of customers do you have?
4 What do your customers want?
4 What would help you to help your customers?
6 What issues do you face in your line of work?
7 Would you be interested in something that could make your life easier?
8 Would you like me to show you our new product?
9 Would you like to hear more about our new product?
10 Do you have a couple of minutes to look at our new product?

Track 70

Speaker 1: Excuse me, sorry… er, do you have any challenges, er, at work? ...Well, I could show you the new mailing system, I suppose.

Speaker 2: Tell me about your challenges at work… Well, then, you need this new mailing system.

Speaker 3: What challenges do you face in your line of work? ...Would you be interested in something that could make your life easier, our new mailing system?

Track 71

1 I'm <u>really</u> sorry, but I haven't got any brochures left.
2 Unfortunately, I forgot to bring my business cards. I do <u>apologize</u>.
3 I'm <u>afraid</u> I can't help you on this. I'll ask a colleague.

Track 72

[beep]

Er, hello, um, I'm just having a look.

[beep]

I run an interior design company.

[beep]

I have some private customers, but mostly it's shops or businesses.

[beep]

They want us to redesign their workspaces and oversee the renovation works.

[beep]

Well, it's hard to get a final decision out of our customers sometimes because the managers are dotted around the world in different offices. This can delay our projects and have an impact on our costs.

[beep]

Yes, that does sound interesting.

Unit 15 Closing a sale

Track 75

<u>For a hard close</u>
How many can I put you down for?
Shall we start the paperwork?
When would you like to start?

<u>For an emotional close</u>
How do you think it will look when it's installed?
What will people say when they see it?
What will you feel like when it's in place?

<u>For an urgent close</u>
It's only available at this price today.
We only have this offer for a short time.
We've only got six of this item left in stock.

Unit 16 Saying 'no' politely

Track 77

1. No, I'm sorry.
2. Unfortunately, that's just not possible.
3. I'm really sorry, but that's not going to work.
4. I'm afraid not.
5. I'd rather not, thank you.
6. Thanks, but I have to say no.
7. I'm afraid I don't really have the time right now.
8. Thanks, I'll get back to you on that one.
9. Thanks, but no thanks.
10. Sorry, but that's out of the question.

Tracks 79 and 80

Speaker 1: I'm really sorry, but I don't have the authority to make a decision on that.
Speaker 2: I'm very sorry, but I'm afraid I have to say no.
Speaker 3: I'm so sorry, but that's out of the question.
Speaker 4: I'm terribly sorry, but that's not going to work.
Speaker 5: I'm extremely sorry, but it's just not possible.

Track 81

…and so that just about sums it up. Shall we start the paperwork?

[beep]

But this offer is a one-off, not-to-be-missed opportunity.

[beep]

Really? But wouldn't you be able to make an exception for an opportunity such as this one?

[beep]

Track 82

And so our designers could completely revamp your website for just $5,000. Shall we set up a consultation meeting?

[beep]

But just think of all the additional customers that a new website would attract. Surely you don't want to miss this opportunity?

[beep]

We could possibly bring it down to $4,500. Would that be of interest to you?

[beep]

Well, that's a shame. But here's my card and if you do change your mind…

Unit 17 The successful job interviewer

Track 84

Mary: Why do you think you're right for this job?

Yiannis: Well, I think that I'd be suitable for the position because I've had lots of relevant experience in my previous roles. Also, I think I'd be a good fit for the company.

M: What do you know about this company?

Y: Quite a bit. I know that it's the second largest advertising company in the country and that you employ over 500 staff.

M: That's right. Now, tell me a bit about yourself. What are your greatest strengths and weaknesses?

Y: Hmm, interesting question. Well, I'm very hard-working and incredibly creative, as you can see from my portfolio. But, on the downside, I'm also a bit of a perfectionist, so I find it hard to let go of a project sometimes. But I'm working on that!

M: OK. And what has been most rewarding about your current job?

Y: That would have to be when an advertisement that my team developed was nominated for Best Local Ad of the Year. It was great to get some acknowledgement for all our hard work.

M: Uh-huh. So why would you like to leave your current job?

Y: Well, I've enjoyed working for a small company and learnt a lot, but I'd really like the opportunities that are offered by working for a large company, for example, the chance to pitch to big clients.

M: Right, so where do you see yourself in five years' time?

Y: I'd like to be working as a senior advertising executive with a number of great campaigns under my belt.

Track 87

[beep]

Well, I've had lots of experience that's relevant for the assistant's position. From what I've learned about the company, I think this would be a great place for me to develop my skills and learn more about the business.

[beep]

Um, I'm very well organized and able to multitask. But I also have a tendency to take on too much, so I'm trying to improve on that.

[beep]

Well, yes, I organized the company conference last year and had to sort out the venue, catering, speakers and so on. My phone didn't stop ringing in the weeks running up to it, but it all turned out well in the end.

[beep]

I've been there for six years now and I'm ready for a new challenge.

[beep]

I'd like to gain experience in all areas of business, perhaps with a view to moving into a junior sales position.

[beep]

Unit 18 The successful interview candidate

Track 90

1 So, could you tell me about yourself?

Candidate 1: Well, I'm 32 years old. I was born in Vancouver but my family moved to the US when I was 16, so that's how I ended up in Washington. I really enjoyed math at high school, so I studied that at college as well. I had a great time while I was there, made lots of friends and really enjoyed the course. Then I got my first job when I was…

Candidate 2: I did Business Studies at Princeton and then joined Kays Brothers where I worked part-time while finishing my accountancy qualifications. I joined my current company five years ago and have worked my way up to audit manager.

2 Why do you want this job?

Candidate 1: I'd like this job because it would give me an opportunity to work for a larger organization than I do currently and so broaden my professional experience.

Candidate 2: Because it pays well.

3 How would your colleagues describe you?

Candidate 1: They'd say that I'm very good at team sports and that I'm always good fun. Just don't ask them what I did after last year's summer conference!

Candidate 2: They'd describe me as a team player, who is always dedicated to getting the job done.

4 How do you cope with working under pressure?

Candidate 1: I don't really like it.

Candidate 2: I try hard not to let pressure get to me and just to concentrate on getting the job done.

5 What is your greatest strength?

Candidate 1: I'm very enthusiastic. I'm always keen to learn new skills and move out of my comfort zone.

Candidate 2: I'm really good at motor car racing.

6 What's your greatest weakness?

Candidate 1: I can be a bit lazy.

Candidate 2: I have a tendency to take on too much, but I'm trying to improve on that by delegating wherever appropriate.

7 Are you a team player?

Candidate 1: Yes, I was part of the team of people who put together a successful pitch for a large multi-national client. We each played our part in putting together a great presentation and we ended up being awarded the contract.

Candidate 2: Not really. I prefer to work by myself.

8 Where do you see yourself in five years?

Candidate 1: I'd like to have retired and be sitting on a beach.

Candidate 2: I like to think that I would still be working here, perhaps as a senior product designer.

Track 91

1 So, could you tell me about yourself?
[beep]

2 And why do you want this job?
[beep]

3 How would your colleagues describe you?
[beep]

4 How do you cope with working under pressure?
[beep]

5 What is your greatest strength?
[beep]

6 What's your greatest weakness?
[beep]
7 Are you a team player?
[beep]
8 And where do you see yourself in five years' time?
[beep]

Unit 19 Carrying out performance reviews

Track 94

1 How do you feel about your performance this year?
2 I've observed that you are steadily improving in all areas of your job.
3 I would like you to establish a job rotation scheme. I expect you to organize this by the end of the month.
4 Down the line, I think it would be helpful for you to develop your interpersonal skills.

Track 95

[beep]

No, I think that about covers it.

[beep]

I think I've done well. I've met all my targets in terms of budget cuts and I think the first phase of the office refurbishment was successful too.

[beep]

Thanks. That's good to know.

[beep]

OK, that sounds reasonable.

[beep]

Yes, I'd be keen to work on that.

Unit 20 Persuading your manager

Track 97

1 I think you'll agree that my proposal for unpaid leave is quite convincing.
2 I'd like to ask for a transfer to a different department.
3 Would you be willing to support my request for extended leave?
4 I'd like to schedule a meeting with you to discuss my position.
5 Wouldn't you say this should be taken into consideration?